PEACE IN
TROUBLED
CITIES

Dafne Plou

PEACE IN TROUBLED CITIES

CREATIVE MODELS OF BUILDING COMMUNITY AMIDST VIOLENCE

Risk
BOOK SERIES

WCC Publications, Geneva

Cover design: Edwin Hassink, based on a poster for the launch
of the Peace to the City campaign by Marie Arnaud-Snakkers

ISBN 2-8254-1256-2

© 1998 WCC Publications, World Council of Churches,
150 route de Ferney, 1211 Geneva 2, Switzerland

No. 84 in the Risk Book Series

Printed in Switzerland

Table of Contents

1   1. PEACE TO THE CITY

6   2. RIO DE JANEIRO

23   3. BELFAST

42   4. COLOMBO

61   5. BOSTON

77   6. DURBAN

94   7. SUVA

113   8. KINGSTON

131   9. TOWARDS A CULTURE OF PEACE

1. Peace to the City

A young man in Boston is fleeing from the gang chasing him. He sees the open doors of the church and runs desperately into the sanctuary, where a funeral is being held. His pursuers follow him. He is not able even to cry out for help before one of the gang takes a shot at him. The rest of the gang catches up with him and is beginning to stab him when the minister throws himself on the youth to protect him. The gang runs away.

About fifty street children and teenagers are getting ready to go to sleep outside the Candelaria Church, in Rio de Janeiro, Brazil. Some look up to the sky and dream of a different world, others inhale glue to forget, still others close their eyes and huddle to keep the cold away. Suddenly there are shouts and threats. The military police have arrived, among them the officer known as "Friday the 13th" because of the terror he inspires among street children. Without provocation, the police begin to shoot. Amidst the cries of pain and despair, eight street children are massacred that night.

Flames inspire fear. The arson attack on the Springfield Road Methodist Church in West Belfast has completely destroyed the meeting room. Two earlier bomb attacks had ruined other parts of the building. Will the congregation be able to bear this third attack? Would it not it be better to close its doors and build a new church in a safer place? Unafraid, the congregation decides to remain. They know that it is right where they are, next to the "Peace Line", that they are called to carry out a ministry in favour of peace in a city divided by sectarian violence.

"The violence at the doors of our churches demands clear and courageous responses," says Rev. Eugene Rivers of the Azusa Community in Boston. "The churches cannot shrug their shoulders at so much violence. We Christians have a clear mandate to work for peace, and we must do urgently."

The Peace to the City campaign was launched by the World Council of Churches' Programme to Overcome Violence in order to draw attention to creative and inspiring ways in which churches, other religious organizations, civil society groups and communities from different parts of the world are becoming involved in joint efforts in favour of peace, efforts that involve finding common criteria and perspectives to respond in a holistic way to the problems that are a part of daily life throughout the world.

"The churches have a lot of credibility among the people," says Angela Stultze-Crawlle, director of the S-Corner Clinic in Bennetland, Kingston, Jamaica. "They are practically the only institutions people trust. They are still willing to hear the recommendations of the pastors and priests. People demand church intervention when there is violence. We should no longer wait for them to call. We have to act in prevention, in working for peace with the residents, the organizations, the civil society, before the violence drowns us." Dozens of ministers and priests have been trained in mediation and conflict resolution to be able to act in situations of violence in Kingston and in many other places throughout the world. They know they will often have to face both victims of violence and those who cause it, and that their words and attitudes could change situations and lives, even though they cannot always expect immediate results.

When Presbyterian minister Caio Fabio D'Araujo Filho visited one of the most dangerous *favelas* (slums) in Rio de Janeiro in December 1994 as part of a campaign against small arms, a 19-year-old young man asked him if he really thought he would be able to disarm the drug traffickers in that area. Caio Fabio responded that "the drug traffickers could begin a dialogue with society if they began by handing over some of the weapons." The conversation with the young man continued, and some of his friends joined in. It was not an easy discussion, but when they finished, the pastor said he wanted to pray for them. The young men accepted. Among those Caio Fabio prayed for was one of the most dangerous leaders of the drug traffic in that area. Unfortunately, he was not able to escape the cycle of violence on time; a few days later was killed by an enemy gang.

Working for peace in cities and communities means working to build a culture of peace. It is not enough to set aside one's own weapons or even for opposing groups to decide that they will no longer attack each other. It means working for a change of mentality, a "transformation of conflict", in the words of Billy Mitchell, a former Protestant paramilitary in Northern Ireland who now directs an organization that works to bring together

Republicans and Loyalists in his country. To bring about this change of paradigm and create the foundations for a culture of peace, all levels of society must participate in the dialogue. In several cities representatives of local authorities, the business community, non-governmental organizations, trade unions, churches and other religious bodies, the media and the neighbours affected directly by violence have been able to sit down at the table and talk. Together they began to search for viable and realistic solutions which take into account the roots of violence and provide concrete responses without creating false expectations among the people.

Working for peace in cities and communities means being willing to include everyone in the work. Men, women, youth and children can contribute significantly to achieving peace in their neighbourhoods and cities. No one is too young or too old to participate in this task. In Belfast, the Corrymeela Community works with children to help them understand why they need to quit stoning each other. In the Vigario Geral *favela* in Rio de Janeiro, an Afro-Reggae band brings together young people who want to stay away from violence and create a new youth identity in the poorest neighbourhoods. In the Valley of the Thousand Hills near Durban, South Africa, Athol Jennings, who is close to retirement, continues to train mediators and counselors for victims of violence and for individuals who need to recover from traumatic situations. In Colombo, Sri Lanka, encouraged by Shanti Satchithanandan of Christian Aid, young widows and their families work in zones destroyed by the war. In Suva, Fiji, Arlene Griffen works tirelessly to involve women more in decision-making so that ethnic diversity and multi-culturalism be reflected in the new political setting of Fiji.

Where ethnic, neighbourhood or sectarian conflicts reach high levels of violence, work for peace involves meditating between politicians and those in power, approaching them so that at least they come to know each other personally – what kind of people they are, who their families are, what their interests are – in order to create a climate of trust that will later enable them to discuss crucial problems. In Colombo, the National Peace Council has developed a series of seminars with politicians from the governing and opposition parties to begin such a dialogue. Meetings are held outside and country and include visits with politicians from other parts of the world that face similar conflicts. The results of this experiment have been positive, allowing new perspectives and generating new ideas.

Violence often arises from or is nourished by economic and social injustice. Proposals for development in which opposing sectors can work together for the benefit of the entire community can often lead to greater success than signing any accord. In many violence-plagued countries the gap between the rich and the poor is a remnant of the former colonial system. In other cases it is the result of the racism and discrimination that persist behind a façade of democracy and equality. In still other cases, it is aggravated by economic measures imposed by international financial institutions which disregard the suffering of a large part of the population when they are excluded from social benefits and access to education, health and decent housing. The frustration brought about by endemic unemployment and the lack of opportunities to improve living conditions nourishes restlessness and violence.

The Peace to the City campaign has focused on seven cities around the world where efforts are being made to overcome different manifestations of violence in a variety of contexts. This book draws on that campaign to share the stories of initiatives from which other churches, organizations and individuals can learn and thus be inspired to do more in their own context to build a culture of peace. When considering each situation, it was important to bear in mind how people have organized themselves to overcome violence, and how different civil society organizations, including the churches, have been challenged to provide a framework for peace efforts by individuals, groups and neighbourhood or grassroots organizations.

Very important in gathering the material for this book was the collaboration of the campaign coordinators in each of these seven cities: Rubem César Fernandes of Viva Rio, in Rio de Janeiro, Brazil; Doug Baker of the Mediation Network, in Belfast, Northern Ireland; Priyanka Mendis, a president of the World Council of Churches and a supporter of the National

Peace Council of Colombo, Sri Lanka; Jeffrey Brown of the National Ten Point Leadership Foundation in Boston, USA; Mike Vorster of the Diakonia Council of Churches, in Durban, South Africa; Amelia Rokotuivuna, a member of the Constitutional Citizens' Forum in Suva, Fiji; and Angela Stultze-Crawlle of the S-Corner Clinic and Community Development Centre, in Bennetland, Kingston, Jamaica. All are firmly committed to peace and have shown a great capacity to work in situations of risk. Without their support and enthusiasm, the Peace to the City campaign would not have had the force and repercussions it has, nor would this book have been possible. It is an attempt to reflect their conscientious work, with its successes and failures, but always looking to a future of peaceful coexistence and understanding in societies suffering from the wounds of violence.

2. Rio de Janeiro

A "House of Peace" on the site of a massacre? It seems unthinkable. Would it ever be possible to rise above the smell of gunpowder and death at the place where military police murdered 22 innocent people on the evening of 28 August 1993?

It took some time for the residents of the Vigario Geral *favela* (slum) to recover from that devastating attack. But today any street vendor can give the visitor crossing the railroad tracks into the heart of the *favela* directions to where the House of Peace stands, colourful and proud. On the spot where a humble working-class family was decimated in its home, the House of Peace has opened its doors as a community centre devoted to developing the neighbourhood and training children, young people and adults for a life with dignity. Its simple lines, decorated with loud and happy colours, stand out amidst the relentless dust, heat and poverty. A modest plaque with the names of the victims recalls the terror of that night.

The House of Peace grew out of the joint efforts of dozens of persons throughout Rio de Janeiro who decided to put a stop to the growing violence that was smothering the city in 1993. Rio had made headlines around the world in July of that year when military police opened fire indiscriminately on 50 street children sleeping beside the Candelaria church in the downtown area. Seven children and one teenager were gunned down. This was followed by the massacre in Vigario Geral, also at hands of the military police. Gangs of adolescents from poor neighbourhoods were invading the beaches of Copacabana and Ipanema. Their vandalism and theft planted fear in the hearts of the city's residents. The middle class felt they had been "invaded by barbarians".

Anthropologist Luis Eduardo Soares points out that Rio was experiencing violence "in three of its mythical spheres: the sacred sphere (the Candelaria church), the domestic sphere (the people killed in their homes) and the sphere of democratic coexistence (the beaches)". The violence risked making Rio an uninhabitable city, powerless to resolve its serious social problems. But how could the situation be turned around?

While many demanded more repression and an even firmer hand from the authorities, a group of citizens decided to search for another answer. It was impossible to keep multiplying confrontations in a divided city that was practically on the verge of internal war. Denouncing the corruption and power struggles within the security forces, they rejected the policy of "shooting first and asking questions later" and called for an end to police impunity. It was important to find ways to resolve conflicts, to raise citizen awareness, to create spaces for community development and participation which could in turn isolate organized crime and the centres of violence.

Peace initiatives

"Viva Rio was born out of passion," says Walter Mattos, a young sports journalist. "This happened at a moment when people were not expecting too much from Rio de Janeiro. Many wanted to move, to leave the city. No investments were being made and the city's economy was going downhill. We were facing what seemed like an insurmountable situation. Crime was increasing day by day and people were scared to death."

It took many telephone calls and visits and a good deal of persistence to get people to join forces and provide a citizen response to the wave of violence. Those were feverish days for this young entrepreneur who had decided to fight for his city.

"I felt I could not continue to live in this city without doing something to change things," he recalls. "I loved my city. My son was born here and I wanted to stay here. I had reached the conclusion that I could no longer tolerate this powerlessness." Walter Mattos's concern led him to contact personalities and leaders in Rio. Sometimes it was difficult to overcome their suspicion and mistrust. But the effort would be worth it if an effective way could be found to put an end to the atmosphere of fear, distrust and social disintegration that had taken over the city.

Finally, an agreement was reached with the participation of leaders in business, the professions, trade unions, the media, non-governmental organizations and social movements. After two months of weekly meetings, all agreed on the need to work together to overcome the violence and to demonstrate that it was possible to integrate the city by building bridges over the social gaps. Herbert de Souza, a nationally respected sociologist who

headed the Campaign Against Hunger, which mobilized the
entire country in solidarity with the dispossessed, assumed the
leadership. The new movement decided to take the name "Viva
Rio" as a way of affirming that it was possible to create a trend
among the citizens to overcome violence, promoting dignity and
equal opportunities for all. Rubem Cesar Fernandes, an
anthropologist at the ecumenical Institute of Religions Studies
(ISER), was named executive secretary.

Among the founding members of Viva Rio were board
members of the city's three main dailies, *O Globo*, *Jornal do
Brasil* and *O Dia*. Mass media support was critical to give
visibility to the campaign for peace begun by the new
organization a few days later. Representatives from different
religious groups were also invited to participate, among them the
city's Roman Catholic archbishop, as well as Protestant and
Pentecostal leaders.

One of the evangelical Protestant leaders was Presbyterian
minister Caio Fabio D'Araujo Filho, president of the
Evangelical Association of Brazil and director of Vinde
(National Evangelization Vision), which owns a biweekly
magazine and a radio and television station. He was encouraged
by Rubem Cesar Fernandes and Caio Ferraz, a young sociologist
born in Vigario Geral, to buy the house where the massacre had
taken place and set up a community centre there. The Dos Santos
family, which had lost eight of its members in the massacre,
were Pentecostals. Jane, the mother, died with a copy of the
Bible in her hands. Only the youngest children had been saved
from death by jumping over the wall onto another street.

The leaders of Viva Rio felt the need to go public with their
initiative. To inspire hope amidst the violence convulsing the
city, they came up with the idea of getting all the inhabitants of
Rio to keep silent for two minutes for peace. They called on the
entire population to keep silent and stop all activities at noon on
Friday 17 December 1993. The movement's leaders went to the
Candelaria church to "embrace" it with a long human chain.
People were asked to wear white clothing to symbolize their
option for peace.

With the help of the media, details were announced and enthusiasm grew. From the outlying *favelas* to offices in the central cities, people prepared to participate in the two minutes of silence. When the moment arrived, what many thought unattainable happened. Rio de Janeiro came to a halt. Traffic in the streets stopped, businesses and the stock market suspended work and trading for two minutes, employees left their offices and people came out of their houses. The streets filled with silent people dressed in white. The Candelaria church was embraced with emotion. There was pride among the citizens that the city had paused in the middle of its frenzied activities in favour of peace.

Building peace without naivete

The leaders of Viva Rio knew it would not be easy to work for peace in a city where the roots of violence were so deep. The economic, educational and social inequalities of the population were more and more evident every day. Of Rio's five million inhabitants, over one million live in slums whose winding streets climb the hillsides on which small wooden houses are built, seemingly unreachable.

The *favelas* are usually controlled by local groups involved in the drug trade or in other illegal activities. These gangs impose their own justice and law on the residents, punishing those who disobey the rules. Confrontations over territorial control with other similar groups are constant, as are showdowns with the police.

Rio de Janeiro already has one of the highest annual homicide rates in the world – 79.3 per 100,000 people, an average of 7000-8000 killings in a 12-month period. Now it is facing the proliferation of small arms, cheap and easily accessible in the local black market. Although Brazil manufactures weapons, most of the guns used by gangs come from abroad and are obtained clandestinely. One can find anything from small pistols to semiautomatic rifles and machine guns, hand grenades and bazookas, as well as the well-known AK-47 or Kalashnikov. With the incursion of the Russian mafia through the Amazon in the north and the Paraguayan jungle in the south, new weapons are streaming into the country illegally to swell the growing arsenals of the gangs. In 1992, the police confiscated 4000 machine guns in the *favelas*. Statistics show that about half a million small weapons, bought illegally, are in the hands of the city's residents.

Police violence is another concern in Rio de Janeiro. Still under the influence of the national security doctrine and headed by a military officer, Rio's police force repeatedly resorts to violence, particularly to subdue the marginalized population. The rigid codes of behaviour within the force resist change. Social scientists say that both the attack on the Candelaria church and the massacre in Vigario Geral were not only an effort to influence public opinion but also a gesture of defiance directed at the politicians and democratic leaders of the police who were trying to bring about democratic and ethical changes in the force.

Important support for the citizens' actions came from national and international human rights organizations. Amnesty International reports point out how the population followed all the details of the investigation, which enabled the courts finally to identify and try several police officers involved in both events. In the Candelaria case, nine officers charged with the crime of killing the street children have been sentenced to prison. As to the Vigario Geral massacre, 17 police officers were charged and tried. But Amnesty International continues to be concerned by regular reports of police killing unarmed civilians under circumstances that seem to suggest summary executions.

Generating respect for citizen rights

Rocinha, with its 100,000 residents, is one of the largest *favelas* in Rio de Janeiro, virtually a city within this big city. Its problems are similar to those of slums throughout the world: unsafe houses, lack of sanitary facilities, little access to educational or health services, and the threatening presence of organized crime in the streets, particularly of the drug trade. At a Methodist church about 100 metres from one of the entrances to Rocinha, Viva Rio has begun several initiatives in which the poor and excluded population can begin to exercise their rights as citizens.

The "Citizen Counters" offer, free of charge, all types of consultations on matters of civil law. People are given information and advice on their rights and responsibilities, assistance with paperwork and legal formalities, as well as courses and conferences on civil rights.

This experiment has been repeated in 19 other *favelas*. Some 35 attorneys and law students, as well as 15 volunteers, work every week at these places. In Rocinha they handle about 30 cases a day. The facilitating and mediating role of the staff is basic in resolving many of these situations. An average of 15 to 20 agreements are negotiated each week. In 80 percent of the cases a solution can be reached at the Citizen Counter; the others are pursued in the courts, with the assistance of staff.

The Citizen Counters work with the National Social Welfare Institute on matters related to pensions, retirement and social benefits. The Federal Psychiatric University receives persons with severe emotional problems, and a Violence Clinic deals with cases of sexual abuse of children. In addition, the Felix Pacheco Institute provides legal documents free of charge. Criminal cases are referred to the district attorney's office.

The main matters dealt with at the Citizen Counters arise from disputes between neighbours over property rights, domestic violence, family law, marriage, divorce and alimony, retirement pensions, workers' compensation and inheritances. If no legal solution were found, many of these situations would probably end up in violence between the parties involved. Through these Citizen Counters, people discover that they can resolve their conflicts peacefully, while exercising their rights. Marlene Da Cruz Geraldo, who is in charge of the Rocinha Citizen Counter, describes the task as "creating awareness that it is possible to ensure that the rights of people are respected within the neighbourhood itself, and that finding just solutions to conflicts is not something strange for the residents of marginalized areas." Even local drug chieftains have sent neighbours here to settle disputes.

For Elizabeth Sussekinde, who coordinates the Viva Rio Citizen Counters, "we need to create a new formal order that takes into account the problems of the poor. The rules for peaceful coexistence vary for the different social groups, so it is important that lower income citizens feel protected by the law."

Viva Cred, which also operates out of the Methodist church's facilities, is a Viva Rio initiative supported by the local Fininvent, the National Development Bank (BNDES) and the Inter-American Development Bank (IDB). It provides commercial loans to give productive small businesses access to the capital needed to improve their activity or business. Viva Cred has granted an average of three loans a day in Rocinha, amounting currently to about US$1.5 million in loans ranging from $100 to $10,000. The low default rate on these loans demonstrates that many people at the neighbourhood level are willing to work honestly at their craft or trade, paying back the loan within the agreed term. Three-quarters of the beneficiaries who pay off their first loan request a second one.

Ruth Cardoso, the wife of Brazilian president Fernando Henrique Cardoso, said during a visit to the Viva Cred office in Rocinha that this type of initiative is "basic in providing a different type of service to the people, which allows the creation of new social policies based on sustainable endeavours that strengthen the unity of the community and defend solidarity." She stressed the importance of "freeing the population from the dictatorship of swindlers" and of small loans as a mechanism for social change in the working community.

A few steps away from the Viva Cred offices and the Citizen Counter is another community service for small businesses, the Balcao Sebrae/Viva Rio. Rio has thousands of small businesses; and this organization provides advice to them on legal requirements, entrepreneurial development, access to loans, participation in fairs and exhibits and training of small entrepreneurs. It also fosters the creation of local commercial and industrial associations and cooperatives, to stimulate joint efforts in neighbourhood improvement. Recycling of garbage, paper and plastics is an important facet of its work. Courses enable children, adolescents and adults to supplement their monthly income through recycling activities.

About 1200 people a year participate in the activities organized by Sebrae. It has agreements with local banks to form support networks for the small businesses and encourage popular loans.

Another interesting experiment in combining community development, citizenship and peace work is taking place in Rio das Flores, on the outskirts of Rio de Janeiro. Here a new neighbourhood is being built for poor families displaced by mudslides following the heavy rainfall of summer 1996, in which 100 people died and thousands lost their belongings.

In Rio das Flores, Viva Rio started a project of building new homes. The families that were moved here have taken an active part in building their own homes through a community system of self-help that strengthens relations among neighbours, creating trust and ties of coexistence. The families moving into Rio das Flores needed professional help to overcome the trauma caused by the floods and the loss of friends, relatives and their few belongings. All must take part in the housing programme. The municipality donated the land and the C&A Development Institute gave the materials to build a basic housing unit, to which residents can add on later. All the homes have running water and electricity. Residents are awarded points for their efforts in building their new homes; and materials are handed out according to this point system. Thus each family begins to value its home, feeling it belongs to them.

The neighbours are also in charge of caring for public areas, streets and places of recreation. A community day care centre was also built, along with offices for health and social workers and for activities like those of the Citizen Counter. The older children attend a nearby grade school. The Network of Exchange of Knowledge, using artisans with different skills, allows the residents to learn from each other and thus increase their employment prospects.

To strengthen relations between residents, groups of ten families were formed, whose purpose is to work together for everyone's welfare. The group leaders form a neighbourhood committee. The names these groups have chosen attest to the pride of the residents in their new neighbourhood: "New Morning", "New Hope", "River of Happiness", "Participation", "New Home".

All this has fostered trust and friendship, setting aside fear and suspicion and overcoming the fragmentation that extreme poverty often creates. "The participation of each resident in building houses and in caring for the neighbourhood has given way to a process of integration, where enthusiasm and a sense of belonging help to overcome whatever problems appear," affirms Baltazar Morgado, the architect supervising the work. "It is very important for the people to be able to see that they can use their own resources and skills to build their own home and to keep their neighbourhood clean and habitable."

For Ana Quiroga, coordinator of social and community services, the participation of the civil society is basic to this type of endeavour. Where state response is slow and bureaucratic, civil society can inspire the work of the communities and support neighbour initiatives. "The task of articulating this at the neighbourhood level is very necessary if we want to begin to overcome daily violence, the violence involved in always feeling marginalized and without opportunities," she says. "We cannot wait for the state to do this work on such a small scale, but it can support the efforts of the civil society and its residents. In Rio das Flores, the municipality learned that there were important opportunities of working with civil society in this type of project. I think they will follow this example in building new neighbourhoods."

Leading a more stable life in their own houses has encouraged many residents to attend adult education courses. It has also motivated them to form a local drama group and carry out different cultural activities at the community centre. They do not want to be urban nomads, but to settle down and have a family life in a neighbourhood where they feel safe and proud of what they have achieved through their determination and working with their own hands.

New goals for young people

Being young in the marginal neighbourhoods of Rio de Janeiro can be dangerous. In the early 1990s the number of homicides of adolescents 15 to 17 years old increased at a time when the number of homicides of adults was decreasing. In 1991, 306 homicides of adolescents took place, in 1992, 424; and from January to July 1993 alone, 348 minors had been murdered. According to research carried out by ISER, these young people were mainly male (90 percent), poor and black or dark-skinned. These were not street children or victims of death squads or of killings. Most were caught in the cycle of violence generated directly or indirectly by the drug trade, which recruits many young people.

Those young people in the marginal neighbourhoods who do not get involved in the drugs business nevertheless come into contact with it daily either through their friends or simply because they live in the same area. Statistics show that more than two-thirds of the murders of adolescents are committed by organized crime. Most of these killings take place near the victim's home. Anders Odvall, a Norwegian volunteer developing training programmes for children and teenagers with Viva Rio, tells how young boys are often afraid of going home for fear of being gunned down in the street or having the bullets pierce through the walls of their flimsy houses during shoutouts between gangs or with the police. Insecurity, fear, mistrust, even terror are daily realities in the lives of these young people.

The leaders of Viva Rio felt it was important to set up initiatives to draw young people out of the cycle of violence. One of the social problems in Brazil is that 80 percent of the population never begins secondary school – which has repercussions for their labour skills and job opportunities. With the city of Rio de Janeiro and the labour department, Viva Rio launched "2000 Community Teleschool", a programme enabling the entire community to be involved in training its young people. Important support for this project came from trade unionists who are members of the Roberto Marinho Foundation, which is linked to one of Rio's main media groups.

A series of educational videos produced by the Marinho foundation, which had been used successfully in training workers in Sao Paulo, became the basis of a unique project in Rio. To begin, students were to attend classes in their own neighbourhood. The state would not provide all the facilities needed; rather, the community's initiative was to play an important role. Civil associations willing to take part were to contribute a classroom with furniture for 25 people and a television set with a video-cassette recorder. The municipality and the labour office paid for the course, which would be implemented and supervised by Viva Rio, who would also hire the teachers, with community participation.

All types of neighbourhood associations and groups offered facilities for the course. Churches, samba schools, cooperatives and community centres opened their doors to the young people; and within two months the entire structure for the Telecourse was set up. In 1997, it began to operate in 144 classrooms throughout the city, with 4200 students. Classes included work in reading and writing, educational videos and group discussions. In nine months, the young people could complete primary school by taking an official examination.

In 1998 Viva Rio began a second formation stage with the Volunteer Civil Service, providing educational activities for young people over 18. This type of service has been described internationally as a "school for peace", since these young people begin to become concerned about issues affecting common well-being and to seek solutions to problems. The programme includes daily classes and a minimum of five hours of community work each week. The 104 educational centres that make up this experiment are known as "Stations of the Future" and the students are "Agents of the Future".

The 3120 young men and women being educated through this service had their first experience in community work in a traffic safety campaign in May 1998 along the main streets of Rio de Janeiro and 32 other cities in the state. Wearing T-shirts with the logo of the programme and carrying banners and placards with traffic signs, the young people made drivers and pedestrians aware of their responsibility on the streets of a city where traffic accidents claim 38,000 victims a year, with a high percentage of deaths.

Young people are also participating in health campaigns, in repairing streets, hospitals and other public buildings, and in environmental work. The organizers consider it important that the young people have an opportunity to educate the community while at the same time exercising their citizen responsibility. This will increase their interest in the community and will allow them to envision a future without crime and high-risk activities. In all, Viva Rio finished 1998 with 13,000 students in these community-based classrooms for young people.

Activities are being developed in Vigario Geral to strengthen the values of black popular culture among young people. The Afro-Reggae Cultural Centre gathers dozens of young people who publish a newsletter, have developed a Web page on the Internet and have formed a popular Afro-Reggae musical group, which represents their neighbourhood in festivals throughout the city. Its success led to an invitation to perform as part of the official cultural events around the World Cup in France in 1998.

Anderson Sa, the 18-year-old coordinator of the Cultural Centre, sees these activities as another way of allowing the community to overcome the violence they have experienced a few steps away from their homes. "We want Vigario Geral to become Vigario *Legal*, where coexistence and respect for other people are appreciated," he states. This project is not a Viva Rio initiative – which shows that other organizations are also concerned about youth in slum areas.

In 1994 Pastor Caio Fabio took on the challenge of creating an educational and community centre near one of Rio's most violent *favelas,* Acari, where an abandoned factory was converted into a meeting place for residents. The factory was donated by two businessmen – one Jewish and the other evangelical Protestant – who also provided the initial funds to renovate it. Pastor Caio Fabio decided that "the factory would not become a pulpit, but rather a place of service" and named it the Factory of Hope, a place where children and young people could find a path to a better future, with training and better job opportunities.

A day-care centre for 158 children now operates out of the factory. The Ayrton Senna Institute, which specializes in information systems, established a branch there, with 600 students; and there is a Xerox training workshop with 257 students. In addition, several unions provide training in different trades. A mother-child health centre and a dental health centre round out the services provided. About 40 social projects are now being carried on there; and it is expected that this will grow to 70 in 1999.

It has been no easy matter to set up and carry out these activities or to deal with the threats and attacks from organized crime, the police or others who see the centre as a threat to their possibilities of recruiting people for their activities. However, Caio Fabio has moved ahead firmly with the project, "holding on to God's hand", as he says, knowing the potential of such a place for encounter and work on behalf of the surrounding community.

Another educational activity intended to integrate young people from the *favela* with the city is the Neighbourhood Gardeners programme, in which teenagers from 14 to 17 get involved in the city by taking care of the plants and the environment. Young people come from Santa Marta, a virtually inaccessible *favela,* many of whose people hardly ever come to the city and feel discriminated against when they do because of their social situation.

"It is important for the kids to feel they belong to the city and to be concerned about and act on the environmental problems that affect everyone: pollution, lack of sewers, piling up of garbage," says Marcia Alves, coordinator of the programme. She works with groups of 20 young people for a five-month period, introducing them to gardening, botany and urban ecology. They take care of plazas and flowerbeds outside the *favela,* encouraging people to begin to trust them and in turn allowing them to feel part of the life of the city. Marcia Alves believes it is important for the authorities to treat the *favelas* as neighbourhoods which form part of the city, and that this requires a significant change of mentality on the part of the residents as well. This project is now expanding to seven other neighbourhoods.

Viva Rio has also developed projects and programmes joining the efforts of middle-class young people from the city with those of young people from the *favelas*. Coordinated by anthropologist Regina Novaes, these "Gener-action" groups are based on a conviction that physical closeness can reduce the social gap and that relations between the groups help to overcome prejudices, fear and discrimination against those whom the dominant culture has marked as "different".

Working with a violent police force

A difficult task carried out by Viva Rio in cooperation with ISER was working with the police force on the issue of police violence, which affects countless people in Rio de Janeiro each year.

A pioneer programme in community policing was launched in 1994 in the densely-populated Copacabana and Leme neighbourhoods, following a model used earlier in New York, Boston, Houston and London. The neighbourhoods chosen had a population of about 200,000 but over half a million people pass through them each day. In addition, there are four large *favelas* nearby. Initially, both the police and the residents were sceptical about the experiment, with many suggesting that community policing works only in small cities.

The process involved direct observation in both police stations and on the streets. The main objectives were to regain a positive image of the police and the trust of the population, to upgrade the quality of police services, to reduce costs through efficiency, to improve the living conditions of the area by reducing crime, disorder and conflict without the use of repression, and to democratize the police force.

Unfortunately, changes in the local government brought about changes in police policies, and the experiment was discontinued after 18 months. However, the evaluation of this period was positive. Street crime was reduced between 14 and 19 percent. The population took part by placing written suggestions and reports in 30 letter boxes located on main street corners, outside of supermarkets and in public buildings. There were no cases of police violence or abuse. The police themselves reported that they felt better as individuals and as public servants. The people began to know them by name, greet them, even come up and talk to them. Their presence was no longer rejected or feared; and they also received help from the residents in solving some crimes.

The new policies, which strengthen the repressive role of the police, have serious consequences for the population. A military officer was put in charge of the Rio de Janeiro police, and his "war on crime" policies emphasize violent confrontation, often lethal, and include neither prevention nor the peaceful resolution of conflicts. Prizes, including promotions and monetary compensation, are given "acts of courage". The winners are police who have participated in shootings and other violent acts. The message is clear: the more violent the police, the more effective they will be.

Attorney Jorge Luis, who works on security, justice and citizenship issues for Viva Rio, points out that this ideology places respect for human rights in opposition to police actions. "The work of the police is measured through its repressive violence," he says, "not according to the intelligence involved in investigating crimes nor by the service provided to the population in preventive tasks. Police work is praised only if it is violent, *winning the war*." Journalist Zuenir Ventura notes that "this belligerent spirit... creates a war that is no good for anybody. The police judge who is an outlaw and nobody investigates. Public security policies are non-existent. The only thing that exists is confrontation."

In fact, such policies are not good for the police either. Jacqueline Muniz, an anthropologist and researcher for ISER, says the police know they are feared and rejected by the people. No one talks to them or wants them close. The people associate the police officer with violence and corruption. This rejection, as well as the low salaries and few possibilities for social advancement, helps explain why the suicide rate within the Rio police force is six times higher than in the population as a whole and so many police suffer mental, heart and alcohol-related problems.

Despite the setbacks, Viva Rio is continuing to work on public security issues and is being consulted by police forces and political authorities in other cities and states. In such cities as Espiritu Santo, Sao Paulo, Salvador de Bahia and Pernambuco, community police policies have had very significant results.

In 1996 Viva Rio developed a campaign against the light weapons which many residents consider indispensable for personal defence, but which cause many injuries and deaths, particularly in private homes and in the neighbourhoods. A new law makes carrying such a weapon a crime. Representatives from the organizations involved in the campaign spent time with people on the streets as part of an educational and preventive effort that proved extremely positive.

In the marginalized neighbourhoods, pastors from the evangelical Protestant churches played a very important role, visiting the *favelas* and talking with the people about disarmament. Caio Fabio organized a successful Christmas campaign which involved exchanging a war toy with some other kind of toy. This made it possible to talk with hundreds of children about the need to encourage disarmament in the city.

In 1998, Viva Rio helped to organize an international seminar on control of light weapons, with representatives from the ministry of justice, non-governmental organizations and groups from other countries working on eliminating these weapons.

The ecumenical response

When the United Nations Conference on Environment and Development was held in Rio de Janeiro in 1992, representatives of various world religions held an ecumenical vigil for the future of the world, known as "Earth Day". Out of this the religious communities in Rio de Janeiro – where all the major religions of the world are represented – formed the Inter-religious Foundation against Hunger and for Life. In two months, this organization was able to raise half a million dollars in donations and create 70 projects that work with people living in the street.

Viva Rio activities on behalf of peace have received broad ecumenical support. The mainline Protestant churches and the Rio de Janeiro Roman Catholic archdiocese are actively represented on various working committees and make their facilities available to Viva Rio programmes. The evangelical Protestant and Pentecostal churches have also taken part in peace activities, particularly in the light weapons disarmament campaign and in educational programmes.

This ecumenism has been broad and informal, without hierarchies or church structures, but with the common goal of working on the most pressing issues for the people, always trying to respond in solidarity and expressing the spiritual dimension of an ethical commitment to society. Andre Porto, coordinator for Viva Rio's inter-religious activities, feels that "working against misery and violence are reason enough for people from different religions to be willing to come together".

Overcoming urban violence is the work of the entire population, according to the Viva Rio leaders and the citizen movement that created it. "No to paternalism and charity; Yes to citizenship," are the words of many of them. That reinforces the importance of stimulating citizen participation in building a more just society in solidarity, with equal opportunities for all.

3. Belfast

"Please excuse the delay, but this has been a very complicated day." Mary Montague began her apology as she dashed into the office. "I've just come from the hospital. My brother-in-law had to be hospitalized with very serious wounds. Last night as he was getting into his car on his way back from some friends' house, he was attacked by a group of men. They beat him until he fell to the ground and left him with a bloodied face. He doesn't know who they were. There was no reason for the beating. Perhaps the only explanation is that he was in the wrong place at the wrong time."

Mary Montague is a community worker for Inter-face Programmes sponsored in Belfast by the Corrymeela Community. What her brother-in-law had just suffered was only one of the countless violent sectarian attacks that have scarred Northern Ireland over the past three decades. For no apparent reason other than belonging to a given ethnic or religious group, people have been physically assaulted, even killed. Still, Mary had come to the office. She had to continue working for peace, working so that attacks like this one on her brother-in-law cease to be daily occurrences in Northern Ireland neighbourhoods.

Locally, this 30-year period of community and neighbourhood violence is referred to as "The Troubles". During this time, some 3600 people have died in sectarian fighting between Nationalists/Catholics and Unionists/Protestants. Thousands more have been wounded. Many have suffered irreparable damage to their physical or mental health. Especially in lower-income mixed housing areas, large numbers have fled the neighbourhoods in which they once lived. Some have been physically forced out when their homes were attacked. More often, whichever group was in the minority locally, fearing attacks from the majority, have retreated to other areas to be "among their own kind".

Although their roots go back several centuries, Northern Ireland's present "Troubles" erupted in 1969, in part due to clashes between Nationalist demands for greater civil rights and Unionist fears of any change in the balance of power. The conviction of more extreme Nationalists, known as Republicans, that force was the only way to achieve their aspiration – an independent united Ireland covering the whole island – gained credibility. This led to support for the outlawed paramilitary group known as the Irish Republican Army.

When the IRA began its open war against British rule in Northern Ireland, other illegal paramilitary armed groups like the Ulster Volunteer Force and the Ulster Defence Association were established with the support of extreme Unionists, known as Loyalists. Of all homicides recorded, 58 percent took place during the first five years of sectarian fighting (1971-76). In 1972 the British government dissolved the regional parliament in Northern Ireland and assumed direct rule from Westminster. This situation has continued until the present, but it is hoped that responsibility for many areas of government will return to a Northern Ireland assembly as a result of the Good Friday Agreement in April 1998. While the conflict over the past 30 years has been primarily between the two factions within Northern Ireland, historian Duncan Morrow says that "there is no doubt that Great Britain is an integral part of the problem in which the Northern Irish are submerged."

Of the fatal victims, 53 percent have been civilian. Many of them died in terrorist bombings. Others have been killed by the security forces during disturbances, like the 14 victims of Bloody Sunday in 1972, when British troops opened fire during a civil rights demonstration in Derry. But most were victims of illegal paramilitary violence carried out in the streets or countryside by extremists on one side or the other. Unlike Beirut or Bosnia, no heavy weapons have been used in Northern Ireland. The violence is the result of deep sectarian feelings that still divide the population in spite of cease-fires called by the main paramilitary groups in 1994 and more recent political developments.

"We are learning that transforming cease-fire agreements into lasting peace unfortunately involves a long and difficult process," says Doug Baker of Mediation Network for Northern Ireland, an organization founded in 1991 to promote the use of third-party intervention in disputes and to support creative responses to conflict in the community.

The continuous violence has led the population to feel threatened and fearful and to lose hope of ever achieving a lasting peace. Understandably, many people involved in peace efforts are exhausted. At the same time, serious violence has often shaken many others out of their complacency to consider seriously the possibility of becoming involved in tasks aimed at building peace. "To support participants in both categories, it is important to create opportunities for people to meet, to build networks and share their ideas, visions and perspectives," continues Baker. "It is important for people to nourish each other with hope, in addition to learning the techniques that will make work in this delicate task possible."

Intolerance in a segregated society

Those most familiar with the situation in Northern Ireland agree that authentic reconciliation will require surmounting the segregation between Republicans/Catholics and Unionists/Protestants which has grown up over 200 years of confrontations and tensions. Only 7 percent of the population lives in truly integrated areas. The majority are in neighbourhoods that are either at least 90 percent "Catholic" or 90 percent "Protestant". Almost all educational institutions up to the third level are segregated; consequently, many recreational activities are also segregated. Although initiatives in integrated education are now receiving government funding, these involve fewer than 3 percent of pupils. For many, contact between Catholics and Protestants happens if at all only in the work place.

Many of the problems facing both communities thus originate in mutual ignorance, as separation nourishes prejudices, intolerance, mistrust and discrimination. In some parts of Belfast, five-metre high "peace walls" divide Unionist/Protestant from Nationalist/Catholic neighbourhoods. Elsewhere the boundaries may not be visible to the outsider, but the local population clearly knows where they are.

Most of the people consulted in a study by the Human Rights Advisory Commission of the Northern Ireland Community Relations Council concluded that a satisfactory constitutional agreement for their country depends less on external issues than on improved inter-group relations between Unionists and Nationalists. A constitutional agreement to ensure lasting peace will not be sustained if the aspirations of others continue to be unknown, suspected or misunderstood. Dialogue across these sectarian divisions is thus essential.

But it is not only social segregation which creates violence. There are also economic causes. In Northern Ireland, 11.1 percent of the population is unemployed. Of all households, 38 percent live in poverty and 32 percent survive on less than £5000 a year. Some families have suffered unemployment for as long as three generations. For a combination of reasons, Catholic men are more than twice as likely to be unemployed as Protestant men.

In the face of this political tension and violence, a great deal of government spending has gone into security costs. According to the Human Rights Advisory Commission study cited above, the British government budgeted £436 million for security tasks in 1994, while a bare £1 million was allocated for work to improve community relations. The authors of a study on *The Cost of the Troubles*, covering 1969 to 1994, correlate the number of deaths in any given neighbourhood with its economic situation.

The bleak economic prospects play into the hands of propagandists for paramilitary groups on both sides, making it easier to recruit young people as fighters, informants and activists. Half of those who have lost their lives during "The Troubles" have been between 15 and 29 (90 percent of them men). The risk of a violent death for a young person between 20 and 24 is 40 percent higher than for a person over 30.

Aggravating the tension and violence are opposing views regarding the presence of British troops throughout Northern Ireland. Many Nationalists view these heavily armed security forces, highly visible on the streets of the main cities during much of "The Troubles", as an occupation army. Their image of the police is no better. The Royal Ulster Constabulary (RUC) is made up of 92 percent Protestants and only 8 percent Catholics. Many Unionists perceive attacks against the RUC as attacks against their own community. Unionist leaders often call for greater security measures as a means of ending violence.

Sectarian violence in Northern Ireland is also nourished by traditions and symbols. Annual marches organized by the Orange Order to recall the victory of William of Orange over James II in the battle of Boyne in 1690 have often led to confrontation resulting in violence and reinforcing divisions. Republicans have used Irish language and culture in ways that have left many Unionists/Protestants feeling excluded.

Creating occasions for peace

The Mediation Network was created in 1991 to help improve community relations among the people of Northern Ireland. "Changes have to take place within society itself," points out coordinator Brendan McAllister. "Along with political negotiations, we need work to make peace more organic in society."

The Mediation Network vision statement speaks of promoting "third-party intervention in disputes and support for creative responses to conflict in the community. After more than a quarter of a century of violent conflict, the people of our society have a deep understanding that fighting about conflict, or indeed, avoiding important issues of strain and division, have not served us well."

The network promotes the idea of working for peace while developing mutually respectful relations within and throughout a divided community. It is an open network, with the capacity to maintain liaison with dozens of private and public groups and organizations. Among its methodologies are facilitating communication, improving understanding, supporting creative thinking, exploring accommodation and reaching agreements. Strategies for mediation include face-to-face dialogue (formal mediation), inter-mediation (when the parties meet separately with a third party who facilitates communication) and mediative behaviour (when a third party provides assistance in conflict situations). The latter two are the most common.

The Mediation Network operates in several different spheres – with churches, with public bodies and politicians, within the justice system, with voluntary organizations promoting justice, peace and reconciliation, and with groups of neighbours and local communities. In offering its services, the organization is clear that it must to respond to the concrete needs of people. In order to be credible it must work with local actors to develop perspectives and skills that sustain their work for peace.

As part of the Local Mediation Project community agents are identified and receive special training to carry out their task of peace-building. "After so many years of confrontation, people have developed their own wisdom regarding the conflict," McAllister says. "We need to take that experience into account and train on the basis of gained knowledge." Developing mediation skills based on local knowledge and experience gives community agents greater confidence in their role and makes them more willing to face the long haul of pursuing peace.

The work of the Mediation Network thus has many facets. It may involve encouraging dialogue between Catholic parishes and Protestant congregations, or training community agents for peace-building in the public or private sphere, or actually mediating conflicts which have a community relations dimension. The work is sometimes silent, which may be essential to facilitate dialogue between political leaders. Other times it may be very visible, as when its representatives have been involved in mediating disputes over contentious parades.

Working for peace in the neighbourhoods

Many cross-community projects in Belfast and other parts of Northern Ireland prove that Catholics and Protestants can live together without confrontation and in a climate of mutual respect and neighbourliness. One is the Currach Community, located next to the Peace Wall that separates the Catholic Falls Road from the Protestant Shankill Road in West Belfast. A few hundred metres away is Cornerstone, another small ecumenical community of Catholics and Protestants. Between them lies Springfield Road Methodist Church. When the Peace Wall first went up in the 1970s, this church building ended up on the opposite side of the wall from most of its members. The only access for them was a small pedestrian gate nearby in the wall or a long detour by car. Because of this inconvenience and the frequent sectarian violence in the vicinity, many members drifted away. Arsonists attacked the building at least twice. But rather than closing, the church joined with the Currach and Cornerstone Communities and the Mid-Springfield Community Association, a local secular group, to embrace a new vision of transforming the church premises into a facility to meet the needs not only of the congregation but of the residents – both Protestant and Catholic – living along both sides of the Peace Wall. They called the new venture Forthspring Inter-Community Project.

After extensive renovations, supported both locally and by the European Regional Development Fund and the International Fund for Ireland, the church reopened in October 1997 and the Forthspring community centre began operations. "It cost us a lot to rebuild the congregation after the attacks," says pastor Gary Mason. "Many were afraid to come back to the church. Thank God, there was a group of members who never lost hope. We now have Sunday School again and nearly 100 people attend our Sunday services."

Members of the congregation, Currach, Cornerstone, and the Mid-Springfield Community Association share responsibility for managing the centre and operating its wide range of programmes: a luncheon club for senior citizens, a drop-in centre, a cafeteria where neighbours can meet informally to get to know each other, three women's groups, activities for children and adolescents. Besides addressing the social needs typical of many urban settings, Forthspring provides a meeting place for peaceful coexistence where neighbourhood residents separated by the wall can share personal stories or take part in handicrafts or other artistic expressions. As time has passed, it has also been possible to set up more structured community dialogues around issues arising out of the peace process in Northern Ireland. "It is important for people to get to know each other, to see that their concerns and hopes are similar and that it is possible to build a community without confrontation," says Noreen Christian, a Dominican sister and member of the Currach Community.

The task is not an easy one. Sectarian attacks continue in the area, mainly from groups of children and adolescents who throw stones and bricks at the houses and over the wall to mark their territorial domain. The violent situation leads many families to decide to move. Elsie Kirkpatrick could not bear seeing her windows smashed week after week and sold her home for far less than its market value. Beryl Kelly had a similar experience but decided to stay and says that there is more tolerance in the neighbourhood now. Whatever the choice, it is always difficult and painful. The two women continue to volunteer at the Forthspring Centre.

Tom Hannon, the Catholic director of the Cornerstone Community, was directly touched by the sectarian violence: during the early years of "The Troubles" his daughter was shot in the street and paralyzed. There was no motive, only the usual explanation: "in the wrong place at the wrong time." Indications were that a "Protestant" group had perpetrated the attack. After the young woman was evacuated to England for treatment, Hannon's co-workers, most of them Protestant, took up an offering so he could go visit her. "The support from Protestant friends at that moment was of great help in helping us to deal with such a traumatic event," he recalls. "Their generosity and attitude of solidarity taught me a lot." Such personal experiences are part of why Tom Hannon continues to be involved in seeking to mediate conflicts in this part of West Belfast.

The Mediation Network supports Forthspring by facilitating meetings of members and staff of the four cooperating groups and has trained some Forthspring staff and volunteers in handling conflict as a way of supporting creative responses to conflict.

In the northern part of the city, where sectarian confrontations also often arise in local areas, Mary Montague carries out programmes that involve people of all ages in working for peace. One of these programmes, carried out along the Limestone Road, one of the 17 "inter-face" areas in Belfast, where Unionist/Protestant and Nationalist/Catholic communities are physically separated by walls, fences or other barriers, made it possible for eight months to pass without violence in the area, after 27 years of seemingly constant mutual attacks.

Mary Montague explains that it is not easy to work with neighbours who mistrust each other, who harbour feelings of anger and revenge for events of the past and who see themselves as the only victims of the systematic confrontations. "People fear each other before they have even met," she notes. "Yet they share many situations in common: the lack of social development of the area, unemployment, meagre family incomes. Both Catholics and Protestants see their own community as the one that has suffered the most, and all of them fear the paramilitary organizations on both sides." Although the cease-fires have drastically reduced armed confrontations, physical violence continues. Besides the attacks on those of the other tradition there are the so-called punishment beatings, carried out by paramilitaries against those in their own districts who they deem guilty of anti-social behaviour. Many of these go unreported, since possible witnesses fear for their own safety.

The Corrymeela Community was founded by Ray Davey in 1965, several years before the outbreak of "The Troubles", with the purpose of working for peace. It is perceived as a neutral organization able to help overcome problems and find paths to coexistence. Its 180 members come from both religious groups, and it carries out its work through two centres – one in Belfast, the other in Ballycastle on Ireland's north coast. Each year Corrymeela organizes about 200 programmes involving over 6000 people, among them young people from schools and youth clubs, persons from churches and inter-church projects, family groups – including those who have been bereaved and the families of prisoners – and other community groups from all over Northern Ireland and beyond.

For many groups, getting away to the Corrymeela Centre in Ballycastle is a helpful break from conflicts in their local situation. The distance and the atmosphere of openness and trust created in the residential setting at the centre often help groups to work on resolving their conflicts and can advance projects aimed at establishing peace across their divisions.

"We begin our sessions with an activity that involves placing a piece of paper in what we call a 'feeling box'," says Mary Montague. "People write down their feelings about living close to the 'Peace Wall'. Contributions are anonymous. When everyone has put in their opinion, we begin to read them aloud. Everybody is surprised to see that the feelings expressed are the same. This shows that there are no differences between what Catholics and Protestants living in such settings feel." Sadness, loneliness, frustration, fear of being hated and discriminated against are some of the main feelings shared.

The session continues with work on identity, acceptance of political and cultural differences, tolerance and the possibility of understanding diversity as something positive. Participants consider possibilities for both communities to become involved in joint tasks that favour coexistence. The Limestone Road residents, for example, put in place a programme called People in the Streets; its coordinating committee includes representatives from each community and someone from Corrymeela.

At the Ballycastle meetings people have the opportunity to participate in worship twice a day. Ecumenical liturgies and unique resources like puppets or dramas are used to achieve a spiritual closeness between participants. It is important for children to take part in these activities, for they are often the protagonists of sectarian fights in school or on the streets, throwing stones at houses or buildings of the other community or lobbing bricks over the Peace Walls. Children are also often traumatized by the violence, so there is also work with them to help heal their wounds.

From suffering to strength

In 1991 a Catholic sister founded the WAVE Trauma Centre in North Belfast. WAVE's main objective is to help people traumatized by the violence unleashed during "The Troubles". Under the motto "Unlock the pain, we are here to listen", a group of eight staff and 25 volunteers work in inter-disciplinary teams to address the aftermath of sectarian violence.

"Since 'The Troubles' began, 600 people have died in North and West Belfast neighbourhoods," says WAVE coordinator Sandra Peake. "In addition to these deaths, we have the 'punishment beatings' and disappearances at the hands of paramilitary groups, which no one wants to report. Most of the people we aid are women who have lost their husbands, children or other relatives as a result of sectarian violence. Many had never been able to talk about their feelings about what had happened to them until they came to WAVE. It was the first time someone listened to them, the first time they were able to feel sure that someone took their suffering into account."

People's emotional responses to sectarian violence vary from defencelessness, isolation and depression to anger about the lack of justice or the absence of a solution to the conflict. Many suffer persistent nightmares, lack of concentration, insomnia or stress as a result of experiencing this violence. Others feel unprotected, impotent or unable to overcome their anger and desire for revenge. Aggravating these feelings is the low credibility of the law courts as a place to find justice.

"Many women in particular are not able to rise above the loss of their husbands or children through actions in which their neighbours were involved – violence carried out by people whom they knew well and had once trusted," says Sandra Peake. "Children and teenagers who have seen their fathers die as a result of a severe beating feel guilty about not having been able to help them. Others have heard a teenager receiving a 'punishment beating' on their own doorstep, but they could not find the courage to go out or to call for help. In the neighbourhoods there is often a threatening climate and self-censorship, so these violent images continue to live in the minds of people for a long time. It is very difficult to overcome terror."

Many of those who have been in paramilitary groups cannot forgive themselves for the destruction brought about by their action.

Sandra Peake observes that being involved in or experiencing violence drives many people to use drugs, alcohol or tranquillizers to soothe their feelings. "Since these are things that have happened frequently, people have the sensation that at any moment they could be the next victim. Often this constant tension also results in domestic violence."

WAVE's committee is made up of an equal number of people who have suffered from violence and of professionals. Their task is to initiate processes that will help to heal wounds opened up by the violence, to assist people in overcoming their traumas, to provide emotional and psychological assistance and to encourage people to express their problems.

Issues like forgiveness and reconciliation are a priority in WAVE. "Often, the people who have suffered the most are also the most willing to pay the price of working for peace," says Sandra Peake. "It is important to know that people can ask for forgiveness and also grant it. It is also important to increase the strengths of people, helping them to quit feeling like victims so that they can help other people who have gone through their same situation. We know there are people whose wounds will never heal completely, but if they begin to help others it means they have begun the healing process."

Reconciliation and community-building

Billy Mitchell was a loyalist paramilitary who participated in serious acts of violence, including two homicides, for which he served a 14-year prison sentence. While in prison he experienced a spiritual renewal and came to see the futility of violence. Believing that having been part of the problem he also needed to become part of the solution, he decided that when he was released he would commit his energies to community work in areas like the one he himself had come from. In particular, he wanted to work on economic disadvantage and bigotry, which had both contributed to his own violent past. That was the birth of the LINC Resource Centre in North Belfast. "There is a culture of violence in our society," Billy Mitchell says. "Actions are carried out that damage the social fabric – like street fights or beatings. But many of the things that strengthen this culture of violence have to do with the frustration created by the lack of response to social needs." LINC thus offers basic work training to former prisoners and others from Loyalist areas with high levels of social deprivation, providing skills for possible employment. Although the centre receives external financial support, its objective is to see the training programmes become self-sustaining.

Liam Maskey, who works for the Inter-Community Development Project of the Newington Carehill Community Association, has a personal story similar to that of Billy

Mitchell. Having dropped out of school at 15 to join a Republican paramilitary group, he also served time in prison. After he was released he too moved away from seeing violence as having any useful role and began to work in the search for peace.

Through a surprising sequence of events Liam Maskey and Billy Mitchell met, and they have become good friends though they remain deeply divided in terms of their political aspirations. The two share a rejection of violence, common ideals for the economic and social development of their districts and an awareness that their own well-being is tied up with the other's.

Liam Maskey and Billy Mitchell are working arduously to create a new climate of understanding and dialogue. They regularly speak together to students, churches and community groups and organizations. Both maintain open communication with those who still have links to the paramilitaries. All their efforts are directed towards the "transformation of conflict", as Billy Mitchell says. "We not only want to change the situation, but transform it completely. Only in that way will we achieve lasting peace in our land."

Part of this search to transform the situation involves meetings between victims and those who have committed acts of violence. "It is important for people to see and know the feelings of the others," according to Billy Mitchell. "In the neighbourhoods, the IRA members and paramilitary Protestant groups know each other well. Everyone also knows who are the victims of violence and who are responsible for these acts. The communities have been placing bombs and killing each other for too long for everybody not to know. That is why it is important to create an appropriate climate now for dialogue." LINC operates a drop-in centre where people can come together to talk and get to know each other.

Although work with former prisoners and their families is not a primary objective of LINC, there is a good deal of work to do in this area. A significant portion of the LINC staff are themselves relatives of prisoners or former prisoners. "We should look at each other simply as human beings who have suffered too much. People should not be stigmatized or discriminated against because of their past if they are willing to change their behaviour and work for peace," Billy Mitchell explains.

He believes that civil society has not been involved enough in the search for peace in Northern Ireland and that mediation skills need to be developed also among ordinary citizens. Thus LINC began five conflict mediation programmes in parts of North Belfast that are known flash-points. In each place two Loyalists and two Republicans were trained to work together. The objective was for people in the same conflict situation, including those involved in violent groups, to begin to talk to each other. These small groups have begun work on the possibility of setting aside antagonism and encouraging coexistence in a pluralist society.

"This is not an easy task," the LINC coordinator acknowledges. "No one wants to take a different stand. They are all afraid of losing. It is important to reach agreements where no one ends up feeling a winner or a loser. Besides, people must understand that we will *all* win if we can overcome death and destruction." People need to go beyond a static understanding of peace and reconciliation and see it as a process over a longer period. "To consolidate the peace process, we need growing understanding and partnership at three levels at the same time: the political one, that of civil society and the neighbourhood grassroots."

"We have learned a lot through this whole task of community rapprochement," Billy Mitchell points out. "We have even learned from the fears we have of each other and from the perspective of people who have suffered. All this has helped us to reach a high level of trust."

The Inter-Community Development Centre where Liam Maskey works also encourages the creation of local mediation groups. The work is carried out mainly with young people, members of political parties and those with links to paramilitary organizations. The centre also supports contacts with people from other regions that have experienced situations similar to that of Northern Ireland. Liam Maskey and other community leaders have taken part in exchanges with representatives from

South Africa and Guatemala about their experiences of the transition from a stage of violence to democratic construction.

"Problems cannot be faced unless one takes into account the main controversies," says Liam Maskey. One of his particular concerns is the future of young people in Northern Ireland. "In the neighbourhoods in which we work, young people tend to be tough and to run unnecessary risks. It is important to work to change their mentality, drawing them away from violence and away from the paramilitary groups and making them the new leaders in the community." Thus he is involved in a programme that includes talks in schools and direct conversations with the young people about the need to work for peace.

Like Billy Mitchell, Liam Maskey feels that peace and reconciliation in Northern Ireland are inseparable from community, economic and political development. If there had been better social development programmes in North Belfast long ago to improve the living conditions of the residents, he argues, it would have contributed to better coexistence.

A shared aspiration of Liam Maskey and Billy Mitchell is the rebuilding of properties damaged by sectarian fighting in North Belfast. Their hope is for mixed groups of workers, with an equal number of Unionists and Nationalists, to rebuild houses that can be sold to both Catholic and Protestant families. By bringing workers together around a common objective, they believe new bonds could be forged among the residents of these conflict-ridden zones.

Billy Mitchell, Liam Maskey, Sandra Peake and Mary Montague have all been part of the Mediation Network's Local Mediation Project, which seeks to support such initiatives and allow practitioners in these programmes to learn from each other.

The churches' commitment to peace

Church attendance and membership in Northern Ireland are very high compared to the rest of Europe. Several denominational and congregational efforts for peace, as well as a number of imaginative local inter-church initiatives, enable churches to play a significant role in reconciliation.

The Presbyterian Church in Ireland has the largest membership among Protestant churches in Ireland, with about 300,000 people in 560 congregations. In 1994 the General Assembly affirmed a statement on "The Church's Peace Vocation", and the denomination's Peacemaking Committee has been setting up programmes to involve congregations in this task and provide them necessary resources. The statement affirms "that to be Christian peacemakers in our situation we must be prepared to meet and talk together with those in our own church with whom we have disagreements, with those from churches whose practices and beliefs differ from our own, and with those from whom we are politically divided". Putting this into practice is not always easy, since most Presbyterians support Unionist positions and many do not encourage ecumenical openness. Nevertheless, all congregations and each of the 21 presbyteries have been invited to designate one person to receive special training as a Peace Agent. Stories of peace-building initiatives by congregations are shared at conferences and in publications.

During the political conversations leading to the Good Friday Agreement in April 1998, the General Board of the Presbyterian Church of Ireland adopted a nine-point plan to contribute to the reflection on this political dialogue. It encouraged its members to become informed, to give priority to interests that are common to all people in Northern Ireland, to look to a better future and to reject any form of sectarian violence bent on creating disorder in the country. It also called for civic awareness on the part of Presbyterians, and invited them to exercise their responsibility in the referendums to be carried out under the Agreement.

Similar initiatives to encourage peace-building activities are being developed by other denominations, and all of the churches have been instrumental in reducing violence by proclaiming love of one's neighbours and the importance of forgiveness throughout the period of "The Troubles".

There are also good experiences of dialogue and exchange among Catholic parishes and Protestant congregations in Belfast. The Belmont and District Council of Churches, which gathers two Presbyterian, two Anglican, one Methodist and one Catholic church, has already celebrated 25 years of joint worship and witness. Clonard Catholic Church and Fitzroy Presbyterian Church have had a longstanding programme of dialogue between their members on religious and political themes and have hosted various inter-church events at which persons from other congregations can explore issues of reconciliation.

About three years ago, Harmony Hill Presbyterian Church and St Colman's Roman Catholic Church in Lambeg began a similar relationship. At the outset they shared acts of worship on special occasions, and each parish hosted the other for some social activities. Recognizing that this had not actually opened up discussions on any of the divisive political issues, they approached the Mediation Network for help. A one-day encounter was planned at a retreat centre in Dromontine. About 80 participants from both congregations talked about their experiences during "The Troubles" and their feelings about the peace process and then reflected on this in the light of biblical faith.

Making space for neighbours no longer to be strangers is one way of laying the foundations for peaceful coexistence in a community. And enabling groups from different backgrounds to take part in what they perceive as difficult conversations is one aspect of mediation.

When the Mediation Network brings together people from different political or religious traditions, it begins by inviting them to share personal stories about their family life and individual experiences, rather than discussing issues. "As a result, human connections are achieved," explains Doug Baker, who is in charge of the Mediation Network's work with churches. "Later, when discussions arise that could lead to polarization, people have already connected in a personal way and are more willing to work through their differences rather than write each other off." Baker recognizes that violence acts as a wedge, splitting apart different sections of the society and destroying good relations. "Our work always tries to strengthen the positive ties that keep the community united, so that whatever could divide it will not have the power to destroy easily what has been accomplished."

About half of the Protestants in Northern Ireland would describe themselves as evangelical. A coalition known as the Evangelical Contribution on Northern Ireland (ECONI) has been seeking since 1987 to address this constituency with biblical insights on peace. Most evangelicals are firmly committed to a Unionist position and the religious convictions of many exclude any possibility of social interaction with people from other political backgrounds. "We work to overcome a narrow-minded view that mixes religion with national identity," says ECONI director David Porter. "Unfortunately, many believe in a kind of sanctification of the community they belong to and the demonization of the other. In addition, the main churches are seen as 'chaplains' of their own sectarian groups."

In 1988 ECONI issued a basic document, "For God and His Glory Alone", which suggests ten biblical principles which support the credibility of work for peace by evangelicals. "In all our programmes we give priority to the work of building bridges, healing and favouring peace and reconciliation," says Porter. "We know there are issues that cause division, but nothing can put a brake on peace and reconciliation."

In its work with groups and congregations, ECONI challenges evangelicals to apply the teaching of the Bible to their political situation rather than using the Bible to support political positions they have already adopted. "We want to have a fresh approach to politics and culture," says Porter. "We also want the evangelical community to renew its trust in itself, rather than retreating into a piety which is divorced from our situation. In the meetings we organize, we invite participants to discover new proposals, to re-examine their positions and to bear in mind new frameworks and points of departure in facing difficulties that do exist."

The monthly meetings of the Christian Citizenship Forum have become a place of encounter for such discussion and biblical reflection on political issues. ECONI's Clergy Forum also provides a place for ministers to come together and share their difficulties ministering in situations of violence.

Christians have founded and are leading many of the organizations working for peace and reconciliation in Northern

Ireland. Sadly, however, as Doug Baker notes, they must too often go outside their own church to find or create vehicles to do the very things they believe discipleship requires in such a situation of division and violence. Many would agree that the real challenge facing the ecumenical movement in Northern Ireland is to reach the churches with the conviction that peacemaking must be central to their own life and mission. The ecumenical movement can also contribute to the work of peace-building – which will be required for many years to come – by nourishing the type of spirituality needed to sustain work for peace over the long haul, knowing that results will not be immediate and that the road ahead is likely to be filled with obstacles and even setbacks.

4. Colombo

About 10,000 persons took part in the Saama Yama peace sit-in in Colombo in December 1996. The call to peace they issued arose from a feeling that they could no longer accept in silence the destruction caused by the war that has scarred Sri Lanka for two decades. For two days, the Vihara Maha Devi Amphitheatre became a platform for peace. Groups from all around the island, including well-known artists, presented popular theatre dramas, songs, dances, poems and narratives on the values of working for peace. The sit-in ended with a vigil and the lighting of candles.

Organized by the National Peace Council (NPC), the demonstration brought together people from all religious groups in Sri Lanka, as well as representatives of dozens of organizations working for the common good. All committed themselves to work to put an end to the war and the prevailing culture of violence, to encourage dialogue and peaceful negotiations among all parties and to petition that money spent on arms be redirected to projects of sustainable development for the good of the people.

These two days marked the first mass demonstration for peace after years of confrontation fuelled by Sri Lanka's dangerous mix of ethnic, religious and political power issues. Gone were the hopes for substantial changes in the internal situation of the country which had accompanied the August 1994 presidential elections, when 62 percent of the voters had supported the peace plan of the People's Alliance and its presidential candidate Chandrika Bandaranaike Kumaratunga.

At the outset the new authorities had seemed to live up to these expectations. It introduced legislation to put into effect the UN Convention Against Torture and Other Cruel, Inhuman or Degrading Treatment or Punishment. It ordered a review of all cases of detention under the Emergency Regulations and the Act for the Prevention of Terrorism. It announced that violators of human rights would be brought tried, victims compensated and a national human rights commission established.

Shortly after coming into power the new government began a dialogue with the Liberation Tigers of Tamil Eelam (LTTE), which has been carrying out an armed struggle for the self-determination of Sri Lanka's Tamil ethnic minority and for the respect of their rights as a people. The LTTE then dominated the northeastern part of the country, whose population is mainly Tamil, from Jaffna, the main city in this region. Government representatives and the LTTE met several times in January 1995 to try to reach an agreement. Then in April the LTTE unilaterally broke the truce, bombarding two navy ships anchored in Trincomalee and killing several members of the security forces. The attacks extended to the civilian population, and retaliation soon followed. Hundreds of Tamils were detained in Colombo and in the eastern part of the country under the Emergency Regulations and the Act for the Prevention of Terrorism.

The government also allowed Muslim and Sinhalese home guards to take up arms. Amnesty International and other human rights organizations expressed concern that handing over weapons to civilian groups would only intensify the violence in the villages and rural areas. Under similar circumstances in the past, home guards had deliberately killed Tamil civilians in retaliation for the death of Muslim or Sinhalese civilians during LTTE attacks.

"This abrupt rupture was a shock for all of us who work for peace," says Tyrol Ferdinands, general secretary of the National Peace Council, which was formed in February 1995. "It was a strong blow to the peace movement, and we had to look for new and creative ways of carrying out our work. We understood that the peace efforts being carried out were fragile, because the structures that had generated the civil war remained intact. The political agreements to put an end to the conflict had not accomplished their objective due to the lack of political will on the part of the top decision-making levels and also of the population in general. The people were left out of the attempts to negotiate a lasting political settlement."

When the negotiations broke down, the NPC found itself as the only institution opposed to the government's policy of waging "a war for peace". Most organizations in civil society agreed with the government that the peace efforts underway had been genuine and that the LTTE had again betrayed the trust and good will offered. By not challenging this "official" analysis of the breakdown of the peace talks, other peace movements in effect gave tacit support to the official policy.

The NPC made it clear that it considered this analysis simplistic and that the only way to put an end to the war was by including the LTTE in the negotiation process and taking into account the aspirations of the Tamils. "This means that the NPC recognized the reality of the Tamil community in Sri Lanka as that of a distinct community," Ferdinands comments. "The NPC was convinced that the aspirations of the Tamils would be responded to adequately only if there was progress beyond multiculturalism towards a significant degree of self-rule."

Internal conflict in Sri Lanka

Sri Lanka is a multi-religious, multi-racial and multi-cultural country. It has a population of 18 million, of whom 74 percent are Sinhalese, 18 percent Tamil, 7 percent Muslim and 1 percent Burghers. The island, located in the Indian Ocean southeast of India, was conquered successively by colonialists from several European countries, who brought their churches with them. The Portuguese arrived at the beginning of the 16th century and introduced the Catholic Church. In the 17th century, colonial dominion passed to the Dutch, who introduced Protestantism and established the Reformed Church. Towards the end of the 18th century, the British took over, remaining until independence in 1948. They brought with them Anglicanism and Methodism. Later missionaries came from other denominations and Christian religious groups. The Burghers are descendants of these three European communities, and most are Catholics. A large section of the Burgher community emigrated to Australia after independence.

The original inhabitants of the island are the Sinhalese and the Tamils, who emigrated from India. The Sinhalese are believed to have come from the Bengal region while the Tamils came from the south of India and are of Dravidian origin. The Sinhalese are mainly Buddhist, whereas the Tamil are mainly Hindu. The Muslims arrived later, as merchants. The Sinhalese speak Sinhala, whereas the Tamils and 90 percent of the Muslims speak the Tamil language. All three helped to build the country and its multi-cultural civilization. From the very beginning, there was much interaction between Sinhalese and Tamils, including inter-marriage.

The strong presence of several religions in Sri Lanka also contributes to its multi-cultural character. Sixty-nine percent of the inhabitants are Buddhist, 15 percent are Hindu, 7.5 percent Muslim and a similar number Christian. Twelve percent of the Tamils and five percent of the Sinhalese are Christians. There are more Catholics among the Sinhalese and more Protestants among the Tamils, but the Christian communities are mixed and have favoured the multi-cultural identity of Sri Lankan society.

Soon after independence it became clear that the British parliamentary system was not adequate for so diverse a society. Despite centuries of peaceful coexistence, the Sinhalese felt that their leaders should exercise power in the island and that Buddhism should be the predominant faith. This idea was reinforced by the belief that Buddha himself had visited the island three times and that one of his relics, a Sacred Tooth, had been placed in the temple of Kandy, the spiritual centre of the country. This gave Buddhist monks preeminence in the political and social spheres.

The Sinhalese also felt that the Tamils had received preferential treatment under the British colonial rule. The educational system introduced in the 19th century to prepare future civil servants concentrated on schools in Colombo and Jaffna, which gave a disproportionate number of Tamils access to a higher education, while the largely rural Sinhalese population was virtually left out of the system. By the end of British rule, Tamils held most of the posts in the public administration and constituted the majority of university-educated professionals. This trend continued over time. By the mid-1980s, 25 percent of those entering the university were Tamils, as were 30 percent of the country's engineers, medical doctors, accountants and scholars.

The Tamils traditionally lived in the northern and eastern parts of the country, whereas the "deep south" was considered a Sinhalese bastion. Over time the population intermingled and for several centuries coexisted without problems. Before independence, the Tamils proposed a balanced representation of all racial groups in the government, with 50 percent of the cabinet formed by Sinhalese and the rest by representatives of the minority groups. But the guarantees for minorities provided by the constitution did not meet the Tamils' expectations. Only one Tamil leader became a member of the cabinet during the first independent government.

In 1954, the Sri Lanka Freedom Party (SLFP) and the United National Party (UNP) established a nationalist policy that was particularly aggressive against the Tamil community. Bilingualism was set aside, and Sinhala became the one official language. Consequently there was a reduction in the number of Tamils able to work in public office and in the security and police forces. A quota was established for university entry which discriminated against the Tamils. Not surprisingly, Tamil youth began to feel that their opportunities for progress were jeopardized. The government took away the citizenship of the Tamils brought in by the British to work in the tea plantations. All Indian Tamils were deleted from the electoral rolls and had to prove their citizenship in order to be re-registered.

The wave of violence unleashed by these decisions shattered relations between the two communities. The support of fundamentalist Buddhist monks for the policies of Sinhalese supremacy aggravated the problems. Although a new constitution enacted under the SLFP government in 1972 was republican in nature, it offered no solution to the ethnic confrontation and extinguished any hope of a participatory democracy in which everyone could be represented.

The declaration of Sinhala as the only official language now had constitutional status; and Buddhism was enshrined as the state religion. In reaction, the Tamil United Liberation Front (TULF) began nonviolent protests and demonstrations against the government, eliciting strong repression. Hundreds of Tamils were rounded up and harassed indiscriminately. Groups of Tamil youth began to react violently. This proved to be the beginning of an armed struggle by the Tamils against the government of Sri Lanka to attain their political objectives. Over the years a number of guerrilla groups emerged. Among them, the LTTE were predominant and are today considered by many Tamils as their "freedom fighters".

In 1976, the TULF declared that the Tamils had the right to self-determination and the need to constitute their own state. The UNP won the elections of 1978, promising to safeguard national integration and unity and to resolve problems around education, use of the Tamil language and access to public posts. But a new constitution promulgated that same year took no notice of these promises and continued to sustain Sinhalese primacy. Violence erupted against the Tamils and was ten times more intense than the previous major outbreak in 1958, when nearly 1000 people were killed. Subsequent reports by investigating committees uncovered clear evidence of advance planning, involving police instigation and organized bands.

As the guerrilla attacks intensified, incidents of retaliation increased as well. The government promoted a colonization of mainly Tamil areas by sending Sinhalese families to take over the land. Confrontation grew. The LTTE initiated a policy of suicide attacks (which continue to this day), for which it recruited very young adolescents, known as the "Baby Tigers", and trained suicide activists, the "Sea Tigers", to attack naval vessels. In recent years, devastating attacks were carried out in the banking and commercial district of Colombo and in the Kandy Buddhist temple by LTTE suicide groups acting as human bombs.

In 1985, peace talks between Sinhalese and Tamil representatives were held in Thimpu, Nepal, with Indian government authorities as mediators. The Tamils presented their aspirations. Though rejected by the government at the time, these "Thimpu principles" summarize the fundamental hopes of the Tamil people in Sri Lanka:

- recognition of the Tamil people as a distinct nationality in Sri Lanka;
- recognition of the existence of a homeland for the Tamils in Sri Lanka;
- recognition of the Tamil people's right to self-determination;
- recognition of the right of all Tamils who consider Sri Lanka their motherland to citizenship and fundamental rights.

An agreement signed in 1987 recognized these principles, but the government did not put them into practice. Growing violence led to intervention by the Indian army, which eventually had to leave the island in 1989 without resolving the problem. Indeed, attacks and human rights violations against the Tamil population increased, and hundreds died or disappeared. The accompanying economic losses were severe. In turn, the LTTE intensified its attacks against government forces and economic interests. There were thousands of civilian victims of communal and rural violence. One million displaced people were driven into refugee camps under very precarious conditions, and thousands of others left the country.

The work of the National Peace Council

The inter-religious movement against electoral violence formed during the 1994 presidential campaign gained firm citizen support, leading to the establishment of a Peace Task Force and a first Conference for Peace in November 1994. In February 1995 the National Peace Council was formed as an independent civic force. With a good understanding of the situation in the country, it made long-term proposals to achieve a just and lasting peace in Sri Lanka.

Within its work for peace and its concern about the serious human rights violations perpetrated by government forces and the LTTE, the NPC measures the human costs of this prolonged conflict not only in terms of the loss of life but also in the perpetuation of divisions, prejudice, hatred and the desire for revenge among the civilian population, as well as the social and economic burdens placed on the shoulders of the people. Also of concern are the militarization of society and the recruitment of women, adolescents and children into the fighting. The NPC has defined its own role as facilitating the political restructuring of the state into a new nation built on the basis of the autonomy, interdependence, equality and dignity of all ethnic groups. Three main ideas animate the organization:

– The only way to put an end to the war is through a negotiated solution.

- A dialogue between all parties in strife is necessary, including the LTTE.
- Any solution must bear in mind the aspirations of all peoples living in Sri Lanka.

Several basic premises have since the very beginning undergirded the work of the NPC. In the first place, history has shown that the responsibility of ensuring a just and lasting peace cannot be left only to the state or the ruling political system. Second, the people should be the main guarantors of peace, and their democratic aspirations must have adequate institutional expression. Third, work for peace that is strong and genuine must be independent of all political forces and at the same time ensure the basic rights of the oppressed.

To carry out its work, the NPC planned programmes at the grassroots level in both the city and the countryside; at the political level, encouraging dialogue and building relations between members of parliament and activists from the different political parties; and at the level of the media, ensuring the dissemination of images and voices expressing the aspirations of the silent majority which rejects war as a solution to the country's conflict.

Nourishing coexistence and understanding

The women began their tale with anxiety. A few weeks ago they had returned with their small children to their village of Dimbulagala, in Polonnaruwa. The houses were half destroyed, the fields had been leveled. One told of how the villagers were beginning to rebuild their houses while looking for ways to survive the loss of produce from their gardens and fields which had been destroyed. She recalled the terrible night when this mostly Sinhalese village had been raided by LTTE forces. Soldiers had gone from house to house killing everyone: old people, adults, children. It was a retaliation attack, since the LTTE accused the villagers of having given information to the army. She and her husband had fled to the nearby jungle with their children in their arms. There they remained hidden for several days.

Although about 50 people died that night and the village was destroyed, this young woman was hopeful of rebuilding the village. She was also happy that her Tamil neighbours had returned. "We were always good neighbours. We even shared food in times of scarcity. I will never understand what happened. The only thing I know is that we will try to rebuild our village and live in peace, accepting all its previous inhabitants, with no discrimination."

The discriminatory measures forced on the Tamil population by the government and the policy of settling Sinhalese families in traditionally Tamil territories have ruptured many communities. The actions of the LTTE and the army have only fed the resentment and violence. For many Tamils in the northeast the only Sinhalese they have ever seen are members of the army and police, since over 92 percent of these forces are made up of Sinhalese. On the other hand, the actions of the LTTE have convinced many Sinhalese that the only thing that the LTTE wants is to exterminate the Sinhalese.

In 1992, eighty-nine Tamil villagers in Karapola and Muthugala, in Polonnaruwa, were deliberately killed with machetes. This attack was in retaliation for an earlier LTTE attack on the neighbouring Muslim village of Alanchipothana, in which 62 people had died. Investigations monitored closely by Amnesty International showed that home guards and police officers from a nearby police post had participated in the reprisal attack against the Tamil village. At the moment of the attack, a local Tamil leader tried to convince the Muslim villagers not to break the peace that had always existed between the two villages. But the inflamed crowd was not willing to listen and the police stationed at the post less than a kilometre from the village ignored the plea for help by the messengers he sent. The Tamil leader's wife and one of his children died in the massacre, and he was seriously wounded.

"The struggle for economic survival in the war zones creates many problems for the communities," notes Rauf Hakeen, general secretary of the Sri Lankan Muslim Congress and member of parliament. "The LTTE forced many Muslim villagers to migrate, leaving them without land. In the Northwest

Puttalam District there are about 70,000 Muslims who live in refugee camps, without the possibility of being able to return to their homes. Many were driven out within a 48-hour period and lost all their belongings." In the northeast, 17 percent of the population is Muslim, in the east the figure is 33 percent. "Negotiations are impossible if the LTTE takes the lands of the Muslim villagers and drives them out," says Rauf Hakeen. "Besides, the LTTE's tax system is very severe. 'The land is ours, the sea is ours,' say the guerrillas. Our people want democracy and they want to live in peace. They have always respected other communities. But it is difficult to move on and overcome fear when lives, belongings and land are lost due to the violence. Those of us who work at the local level with the villagers know that achieving peace is a long process."

In Polonnaruwa, the NPC supports the Institute for Social and Human Advancement (INSHA), which began working in 1992 to address the neighbourhood violence which had taken nearly 3000 lives in a ten-year period. Lalith Pushpaskumar, who heads the organization with his wife Wasanthi Jayasiri, says that they devoted six months to study why the communities in this area were so fragmented. They concluded that the basic motive for the tensions between the Tamil, Sinhalese and Muslims is not ethnic, but rather the action of external political forces. Government measures and LTTE attacks had fed these tensions over the years. "We decided to begin the task by focusing actions on the long tradition of good relations that had existed before the conflict," says Lalith Pushpaskumar. "In this area, with about 6000 inhabitants, there are many mixed marriages and communities used to visiting each other, eating and drinking together in a show of hospitality. We stress the need of continuing these relations, building unity and strengthening already existing ties." INSHA's objectives are to assist the rural population in attaining economic goals, facilitate peaceful coexistence and work alongside other organizations to overcome the situation of abandonment and poverty. With its ten community workers, INSHA has been able to reach agreements with government sectors to carry out its task.

When INSHA started, Lalith Pushpaskumar continues, "the communities were scattered in refugee camps outside their place of origin. The main problems were to survive and to achieve respect for the dignity of all people. The tension and insecurity that exist in zones that border the provinces at war made this difficult. It was important to receive support from the NPC. Their experts formed small groups of villagers who were willing to produce together and exchange their products." In an area where there are only limited possibilities of obtaining food and other goods, being able to exchange with each other or join together to buy products elsewhere has helped to reduce the tension. It was necessary to give the population a sense of stability, of safety at work and of the possibility of being able to market their products.

By the end of a year, the communities could see concrete results from their work and began to feel they could survive the destruction caused by the war. Their growing confidence in INSHA increased their readiness to be involved in actions for peace, understanding the situation other villages like theirs were going through. They became aware that they could work together without animosity. And, says Lalith Pushpaskumar, "they also discovered they have something in common: they all believe in divine assistance. So they decided to celebrate the harvest together with a religious ceremony – the first festival they had after ten years of division."

Although retaliatory violence has ceased between the communities, the people continue to suffer attacks because of their location in a border zone. The actions of the security forces and of the LTTE have not ceased. In spite of this, other organizations have followed the example of INSHA.

Seeing what has been accomplished, the villagers now want to have a cultural event to attest to the fact that peace is possible. They have suffered greatly. Many of them are orphans or widows, many have seen their loved ones killed violently. Some of the women have been raped in the attacks. But the improvement in the economic and social situation has made the villagers are willing to work for a better future, rebuilding trust between the communities, overcoming the losses caused by the war and re-creating bonds of friendship that help them feel safe.

The situation is no better in the eastern province, dominated by the LTTE, where the land has become a battlefield between the army and the rebel forces. The non-governmental organization MANDRU, in Batticaloa, works with communities living under constant war. On the one hand, the LTTE demands their belongings and products to keep its soldiers going; on the other hand, the army, which suspects that every Tamil villager is a potential LTTE collaborator, requires all kinds of work and products from the villagers, again without any payment. Reports of harassment by army soldiers of younger women increases the villagers' concern for their safety.

The reality of these communities is summed up well by a Tamil villager at a meeting with NPC representatives: "The people live in terror. They are afraid of being beaten, killed or simply disappearing at the hands of the army. They fear that their young people, due to the lack of possibilities, will join the LTTE after hearing a fanatical speech. Many adolescents and even children join this force and become part of the suicide commandos that are responsible for the bombings. We are afraid of the bombs, of the requisitions, of losing our mental stability. We feel our lives are not worth anything."

The villagers also resent the government policy of bringing Sinhalese farmers in to take over their lands. They feel that media reports of what is happening present a biased version which does not fairly take account of the situation of the Tamil population. The fact that they are not able to sell their crops adds more worries.

Engaged alongside MANDRU in community development work in Batticaloa is the Jeeva Jothy Children's Home, which began aiding war orphans six years ago. Thousands of children have lost their parents during the armed struggle, many of them in this region. There are also thousands of widows. Jeeva Jothy is organized around foster homes in which children live as if they were part of a family. This safe environment makes it possible for them to continue their schooling, receive psychological help and lead lives that are as normal as possible.

In some villages theatre is being used in the work for peace. During the 1980s both the LTTE and the government used dramas, songs and the media in their propaganda. Heroic songs and plays extolling militarism were common. Now groups are giving workshops on how to use popular drama to get villagers to express their concerns and overcome the traumas caused by the war. K. Sithamparanathan, a professor of drama and theatrical arts in the University of Jaffna, and A. Sathasivam Paskaran, also from Jaffna, work together in the Theatre Action Group, with its headquarters in the northeast. They organize five-day workshops in villages where participants can express their emotions through spontaneous dancing, music and songs, using the rituals, symbols and techniques of traditional Sri Lankan drama. Participants make their own costumes and masks and use paints made of seeds and leaves.

"Sometimes we have up to 100 people at a workshop," says K. Sithamparanathan. "We feel that popular dramas express the community and allow us to come very close to their psychological and spiritual needs. People are willing to speak with their hearts in their hands." After the dramatizations, the people begin to talk and, with the help of an interdisciplinary group of professionals, including persons from the university's psychology department, community ties destroyed by the war begin to be re-established. "Music plays a vital role in animating the people. Often, the war is represented through dancing. It is important to allow people to feel free to express themselves. Later on we can reflect about it."

K. Sithanparanathan says that "it is very difficult for a Tamil to understand the official discourse of a 'war for peace'. It is as if they are being told, 'We are killing you to help you.' This offends their feelings. So it is not easy to work for mutual acceptance and respect between the communities. The Tamils need their rights for equality and justice to be recognized. If the terms for a just peace are accepted, with equal rights for all, all of the communities in Sri Lanka could continue living together without problems."

In 1997 the NPC began to develop a process of discussion and dialogue with people throughout the country, leading to the

National Peace Delegates Convention at the Bandaranaike Memorial Conference Hall, in Colombo, in early January 1998. Since the government had already launched a new peace plan based on what it called a "Devolution Package", many mistakenly anticipated that the convention would focus on this. But the Devolution Package has been criticized by the peace movements for several reasons – one being that it was created without consulting the LTTE. Many felt that the sentiments of the ethnic and religious minorities were not reflected adequately in the proposed package. For this reason, the convention took as its theme "Divided by War, United by the Cry 'Don't wage war on my behalf'".

A good deal of preparatory work was carried out through dialogues for peace in countless villages all around Sri Lanka and through a major publicity campaign. A "Cost of War" report was published, giving the real figures of human and economic losses caused by the prolonged confrontations on the island and the devastating consequences for the poorest. The convention thus attracted attention from the media and the public at large. Eighteen hundred people, far more than expected, gathered in Colombo in a demonstration of the unity of their commitment to peace. Almost 60 percent of the delegates were women and there was a good number of young people.

Messages to the Convention came from the government, opposition parties and the LTTE. The final declaration states: "We jointly resolve that this civil war is a crime against humanity and society and hereby demand that both the government and the LTTE make a serious and determined commitment to end this war immediately and to establish the appropriate structures and mechanisms in order to achieve a just and lasting peace through a negotiated political settlement."

The role of religion in the peace process

Many people in Sri Lanka, particularly among Tamils, feel that the Buddhist monks display an intolerance for minorities that verges on fundamentalism and that they are creating obstacles to peace so as not to lose the supremacy of their religion on the island. In fact, a significant number of young

Buddhist monks are open to dialogue and do favour recognition of Sri Lanka as a multi-ethnic, culturally and religiously pluralist country in which the rights of all groups are admitted.

Many Buddhist believers deplore the fact, although about 40 percent of the monks seriously favour dialogue and work for peace, the priests in charge of the main temples are very fundamentalist in their preaching and have an influence over government decisions with their inflamed discourse. They also point to hidden economic interests: some Buddhist believers wish to maintain Sinhalese supremacy and are thus ready to pay Buddhist priests to visit the villages to stir up believers against the Tamil.

But just as fundamentalist priests visit the villages to impart their teachings, so do those priests who support peace; and their testimonies indicate that most of the grassroots population accepts peaceful coexistence. These monks feel that Sri Lankan Buddhism should return to its roots: the practice of nonviolence, peace-building, respect for life and the belief that all people are equal, rejecting caste and racial superiority.

Although Christians are a small minority in Sri Lanka, the churches and the ecumenical movement have had an influence through their witness for peace in a convulsed society. The National Christian Council (NCC) has carried out important work in inter-faith dialogue, working with the Interreligious Peace Foundation (IPF) and the Catholic Justice and Peace Commission to organize meetings between Buddhists, Hindus, Muslims and Christians. The visible participation in these encounters of priests and ministers from different confessions has had an important symbolic significance.

Meeting together has often led to actions by these three organizations. "We must begin by speaking with the priests and ministers of the different religions," points out Rev. Rienzie Perera, former general secretary of the NCC. "For this, we have participated in seminars in which we have tried to understand the different perspectives on the conflict, to improve relations among ourselves and to see how we can intervene in conflict situations at the local level. Religious leaders must be the first to be educated for peace."

These programmes are aimed at clergy and lay people of all faiths, and take the form of two-day seminars in different parts of the country. Usually about 40 to 50 people participate. The issues most often discussed are how religious leaders cope with a militarized culture and work with a population very much involved in war and violence against its neighbours.

Another educational programme is aimed at high school students, who are often exposed to propaganda from both the LTTE and government military recruiters. A pilot project in Colombo, using artistic and literary competitions, was later expanded to six other places. The participation of Buddhist monks in organizing it helped to ensure that the programme was well received in the schools.

The programmes, a dozen of which were planned for 1998, each with 200 students, are in both Sinhalese and Tamil. NCC leaders hope this work for peace among the students will lessen the attractiveness of recruitment efforts by the parties at war and reduce the number of young people drawn into the violence.

Vasanthy Rajaratmam, secretary for the Church of South India Jaffna Diocese, carries out a ministry for peace and reconciliation in the Batticaloa region. Supported by UNICEF and private donations, she works with mothers between 18 and 40 who are living with their children in situations of poverty due to the war. Many are themselves war widows with very little job training, for whom survival in a hostile environment is a constant struggle.

The programme includes elements of work training as well as psychological and spiritual support to overcome the consequences of the violence that has destroyed their homes and the lives of their loved ones. The women can obtain small loans to begin cultivating their lands or to produce food or merchandise for sale. Two day-care centres provide care for 90 children while their mothers work. The women come to the church once a week to participate in a health course, a time when they can also support each other. In all, the Church of South India Jaffna diocese operates 87 day-care centres, 12 orphanages and a home for persons with mental disabilities.

"The people in the community are willing to do volunteer work," says Vasanthy Rajaratnam. "Usually they feel a large responsibility towards their community. In spite of their vulnerability, these villagers are very generous. I do not find any hate against the Sinhalese. That is why I feel it is important to strengthen relations between priests and ministers of the different religions. They help to overcome religious intolerance and suspicion. I think that among the younger generations there is more awareness of the need to put an end to the discrimination that keeps the communities apart."

Rev. Duleep Fernando, president of the Methodist Church of Sri Lanka and the NCC of Sri Lanka, feels that it is important for the Christian churches together to support the dialogue for peace and reject military solutions. His church is very much present in the conflict areas, providing emergency aid with the support of international organizations. It also operates 30 day-care centres, 90 pre-schools and 15 children's homes, and carries out educational work with young men and women, providing job training in electronics, automobile mechanics, leatherwork and sewing for some 200 students at the Eastern Technical Institute. Small generators have been installed in many churches, so that young people can go study there when there is no electricity, which has been rationed due to the war. During the long siege of Jaffna, which was recaptured by government forces in 1997, two Methodist churches were destroyed in the bombings, and the Methodist hospital was struck, killing nine people.

Shanti Satchithanandan, a member of the NPC Board who also works in community development in the tea plantations in the central part of the country, says that in northern and eastern Sri Lanka, where the war is harsher, relations between non-governmental organizations and the security forces tend to be hostile. "What aid organizations want to do is to relieve the communities affected by war and help them to organize and overcome the situation of poverty they are in. The farmers want to secure their land, but they feel their opinion does not count and that their rights are of little importance. Because of this, it is important for us to work in fostering community organization and in encouraging local leaders. The workshops organized by the NPC in the communities are aimed at formulating a peace plan for the zone. We also pay a lot of attention to the problems among young people, because we know that often their frustrations lead them along the path of violence. It is important to have facilitators from outside the community who can act as mediators and trainers in resolving conflicts."

Encouraging dialogue among politicians

One of the most striking NPC programmes seeks to promote dialogue for mutual understanding between politicians of different political parties as a way of beginning conversations towards a just and lasting peace. More than 20 members of parliament have taken part in a series of activities intended to show them first-hand how peace settlements have been reached in other countries, including the Philippines, Northern Ireland and South Africa.

In these meetings and visits the politicians have been able to speak directly with the protagonists of the peace dialogues and thus to see the possibilities for similar negotiations in Sri Lanka taking into account the rights of all parties involved. "In our country there *are* good possibilities for peace," says Rukman Senanayake, a UNP member of parliament who participated in these NPC seminars. "The people have lived together for centuries, so it is possible to rebuild the ties broken by this war. The next generations will probably do so, and we will have to learn to work as a team, to accept the help of facilitators, mediators and guarantors and also to recognize that we cannot move ahead without the participation of LTTE representatives in the negotiations."

D. Siddhathan, a leader of the People's Liberation Organization of Tamil Eelam (PLOTE), says that "it was good to be able to participate in these seminars with representatives from other parties, since it helped us to get to know each other and to see that it is possible to relate as persons, in spite of our political divergence." Although there will always be rivalry between us, I think we can have a positive dialogue with the help of good mediation."

Dulles Alahapperuma, a member of parliament for the People's Alliance, was impressed by the way both main parties in South Africa had continued to negotiate even in the midst of violence. He also felt the experience of Northern Ireland, where the paramilitary groups were not asked to set their arms aside to begin the peace talks, was important. Sarath Amunugama, a member of parliament for the UNP, also underscores the importance of promoting interaction between politicians. "We are not all open to the possibility of new ideas. Therefore, we must move delicately; and in this the NPC is with us, offering these opportunities to find out about new trends in the negotiation for peace."

The NPC also encourages meetings between local politicians. In April 1998, a group of Sinhalese politicians from the district of Matara in the south visited their counterparts in the district of Batticaloa in the east. The visitors belonged to the ruling party and the UNP. All had earlier participated in awareness-raising workshops on the relations between the communities and the National Peace Delegates Convention. However, this was the first time that the Sinhalese politicians had visited an area of Tamil majority. With help from the NPC, they simulated a peace resolution, arriving at the conclusion that a combination of sincerity, political will and dialogue can lead to mutually acceptable commitments. At the end of the meeting, a working committee was formed to expand this process to local governments throughout the country.

When people become aware that they have the capacity to contribute to peace, their confidence and willingness to work together grows. Working for peace in Sri Lanka has a great deal to do with getting people to meet to understand the life-style, ideas and hopes of others. In this way they will feel called to join efforts in favour of peace.

5. Boston

By the year 2006 there will probably be about 30 million adolescents in the United States – the highest figure in proportion to the rest of the population since 1975.

Many people in the United States view this growth as a cause for concern. In 1995, the National Research Council's Panel on High-Risk Youth reported that nearly one in four of the 7 million young Americans between 10 and 17 were at risk of not being able to achieve a productive adult life. The panel warned that the US was in danger of losing a generation of children and adolescents from low-income families who abuse illegal drugs, become involved in unsafe premarital sex, cannot find or keep a job and commit or are victims of all types of crimes, some very serious. One explanation of all this offered by the panel is that "no good models for teenagers" exist in the neighbourhoods where they grow up. On the contrary, "many adults involved in illegal markets live there. The poorest neighbourhoods are less and less able to set limits on criminal or deviant behaviour."

Although the consumption of crack cocaine has dropped significantly overall in recent years, its use continues to be high in the inner cities of the east coast, along with a range of other drugs, including heroin. In several large eastern US cities, the percentage of teenagers using illegal drugs in 1996 was more than triple that of 1990.

In 1997 the Council on Crime in America urged that "the challenge in preventing crime in the United States – which is really a challenge in reaching young people at high-risk with an adult presence – be faced, and soon". There were 2.7 million arrests of minors under 18 (a third of them under 15) in 1994, a million more than in 1991. Minors were responsible for about 14 percent of all violent crimes and 25 percent of all felonies against property reported by the police. Adolescents accounted for 26 percent of the increase in violent crimes from 1985 to 1994, including a 50 percent increase in thefts, 48 percent in rapes and 35 percent in homicides.

"With these figures in mind, we have launched Operation 2006, with a call to the churches to become actively involved in the work with inner-city youth, who form a large part of the young population at high risk," says Eugene Rivers, an African American Pentecostal minister of the Azusa Christian

Community of Boston. For this campaign Rivers, who is one of the founders of the Boston Ten Point Coalition and currently chair of the National Ten Point Leadership Foundation (NTLF), has achieved a broad consensus among the African American churches in his city, as well as among churches in cities that have begun to join the NTLF.

Additional support has come from professionals and scholars, including criminologist John DiIulio Jr of Princeton University. For DiIulio, this involvement of the churches is critical, because no one else can deal holistically with the material and spiritual dimensions of the problem. "They are also capable of doing it in a way that is unapologetic about the unconditional love that motivates it. You have pastors that can say, 'The world may hate you, but I love you. God has something better for you. I don't want you using drugs; there is something better for you out there.'"

"We have to rebuild the church around the poor," adds Rivers. "For this, it is important that we unite to coordinate strategic actions for Operation 2006. We believe that if 50 churches join together in a city to work, it will be enough to put a stop on teenage violence and to move ahead with new proposals for youth." Among other things, this campaign plans to work with probation officials and to monitor police actions, collaborating in preventive tasks and avoiding police violence against African American youth. Rivers calls the church "a sleeping giant. It has the duty to become involved in this task and certainly the results will be impressive."

Operation 2006 is aimed primarily at African American, Latino and other ethnic minority youth who live in the inner cities – statistically the group at highest risk. According to a recent study, only 43 percent of young African Americans in the inner cities are reared by both their parents; only 29 percent can count on the regular presence of an adult male figure in their homes; only 26 percent have employed adults in their families; 31 percent are unemployed; and 36 percent use drugs. While the number of homicides decreased in 1995 the figure remained high among young African American males. Although they make up only one percent of the total population of the US, African

Americans between 14 and 24 committed 30 percent of all homicides and were victims of 17 percent.

The purpose of Operation 2006 is not only to prevent crime but also to establish links between the churches, youth and the community, and to begin a new model of relationships characterized by mutual assistance, peaceful resolution of conflict and the establishment of norms for coexistence and participation so that neighbourhoods become safe places where it is possible to lead a normal life.

Forming the Boston Ten Point Coalition

The young man fled from his pursuers, who were chasing him with automatic weapons. Seeing the church doors open, he ran in to find shelter, but the gang chased him around the sanctuary, shooting up the church in the process. Just as the young man would have been stabbed to death, the minister threw himself on him to protect him. The gang ran away.

This tragic episode took place during a funeral at the Morning Star Baptist Church in Boston in 1992. The minister and congregation – indeed the whole Boston community – were stunned. Many were shocked that a "sacred place" had been violated. But Eugene Rivers said it clearly: if the churches were not willing to go out to the street, the street would come in to them. Urban violence would continue to knock on their doors.

Afterwards, a group of ministers from different churches, most of them African American, decided to organize and work together to deal with the problems of youth from racial minorities at high risk. They formed the Boston Ten Point Coalition, aimed at putting a stop to drug use and destructive behaviour by youth and at making local congregations more effective in rebuilding the social fabric of the community in collaboration with the government, neighbourhood organizations and the private sector. The name of this ecumenical coalition came from their "10-Point Plan to Mobilize the Churches":

1) foster church collaboration in sponsoring "Adopt a Gang" programmes to organize and evangelize young people involved in gangs;

2) commission missionaries to accompany young African Americans and Hispanics in court and work with the probation officers and school principals to develop tasks aimed at high-risk teens and their families;

3) prepare street workers to help in the recovery of young drug addicts;

4) establish economic development projects with community participation;

5) establish mutual support links between suburban and downtown churches and ministries;

6) initiate neighbourhood crime-watch programmes in the areas around churches;

7) establish relations between the churches and health centres;

8) promote the work of African American and Hispanic women and men on issues related to family responsibility and alternatives to the gangs;

9) establish crisis centres in the churches to help women victims of domestic violence or rape;

10) develop identity programmes in the churches to help African American and Hispanic people to value their own cultures and appreciate the value of the struggle of women, men and the poor for the dignity and freedom of their peoples.

The Ten Point Coalition urged churches, their agencies and the theological community to consider, discuss and implement any or all of these points.

The first approaches were not easy. The ministers decided to go out on the streets in groups of three or four late on a Friday night and to visit the areas where they knew there were gangs. The behaviour of the ministers initially caused some suspicion. The police thought they might be involved with drug traffickers; the dealers thought the police had sent them. On one occasion Rivers' house was shot at. But little by little, the young people and ministers began to talk and establish trustful relationships. What the young people mostly wanted was to be able to talk with an adult willing to listen to what they thought and share their daily problems. Gradually the ministry began to gain more support.

The ministers of the Ten Point Coalition believe that most churches do not realize how much spiritual and practical power they have, especially together. For instance, if 200 churches in Boston could keep only their own four corners free of violence, this would mean that 800 city corners would become livable again, encouraging community development. On the basis of his research into the causes of crime in the USA, John DiIulio emphasizes "the four M's" for overcoming juvenile violence: monitors, mentors, ministers and moral precepts. "Young people need and have a right to be taken care of by an adult," he says. "Any day of the year there are an average of half a million cases of juveniles on probation. These kids need someone to advise or help them, and they are not finding that. Those who need to be confined in a safe institution are not. The system has no credibility. There are many kids who need a kind of big brother or sister to guide them in a holistic way. And this holistic approach can only be provided by the churches through a specific ministry that takes into account both material and spiritual needs."

The coalition established contacts with police, probation officers, school principals and the general public, especially through neighbourhood organizations, to involve citizens in the task of drawing young people away from criminal circles and drug use. The sharp decline in teenage victims of violence in the inner city streets was recognized by US Attorney General Janet Reno and President Clinton on a visit to Boston. The years 1996 and 1997 marked an important success for citizen efforts, since there was no violent death among young people under 16 until one young boy was killed towards the end of 1997. The Coalition now has more than 50 member churches and organizations and numbers among its collaborators the Jewish Community Relations Council, the US Attorney's Office, the US Department of Justice and Cardinal Bernard Law and the Catholic archdiocese of Boston.

The African American ministers leading this movement are convinced of God's presence in this ministry. Coalition chairman Ray Hammond said that while many have spoken of "the Boston miracle", he feels it should be called "the miracle from God in

Boston". "As members of the Coalition we have seen how, with God's help, a difference has been made in the lives of many young people. We have seen what faith, prayer and fellowship can do. This pushes us to move on, because there are still many gangs to adopt, many streets to recover and many families to strengthen. We must train young ministers, we must continue to pray and proclaim salvation."

Work with young people at risk

A Gallup study highlights the good reputation of the African American churches. In this country where 96 percent of the population professes to believe in the existence of God and almost 70 percent of all adults say they are members of a religions group, about 43 percent of the population attends services each week. Among African Americans, the figures are even higher: 82 percent are members of a church and a similar number indicate that religion has an important place in their daily lives. In addition, more than 80 percent believe that the churches and religious practice can be effective in resolving social problems.

Thus it is not surprising that when the African American ministers decided to form the Boston Ten Point Coalition, they found significant grassroots support in their churches. In addition, they began to work with middle-class African Americans, appealing to their responsibility as citizens and sense of solidarity towards the least favoured of their race. "I believe that the African American churches have a big responsibility in relation to what is occurring with young people of our race in this country," says Eugene Rivers. "If we do not act now, the rest of the population will begin to demand of us: what have you done for your young people?"

Besides themselves going out on the streets to meet with groups of young people every Friday evening, the ministers have sponsored street workers. In cooperation with the churches, police authorities and probation officers, these street workers constantly monitor and follow up on the activities of the young people in the streets. They have become an important point of reference for the entire population, since they are ready to help, give advice and find solutions to any problems.

Teny Goss is a street worker with the Azusa Christian Community, located in the Four Corners neighbourhood in the suburb of Dorchester. This Pentecostal fellowship set up its meeting place in a half-destroyed "crack house" which had been used by a gang of drug traffickers. The members of the community considered it their witness to convert what had been a den of delinquency into a place where families, children and young people could find support, spiritual guidance and people willing to help them to address their needs.

Every day Teny Goss drives through the streets of the neighbourhood, where he knows all the youth by name. He relates to school authorities, the police and the probation officers, but his task is mainly to help mediate, provide guidance and support. "I think it's important to know that these kids can become successful citizens if one helps them to grow up with positive values," he says. "From all these years of work, I have found that they want to improve, to build up their lives and work towards that. But they need guidance from adults willing to direct them along the right path. These kids want adults also to be responsible. When we realize that we live in the democracy with the most people in prison, we should be asking ourselves what we need to do to change that situation in a more profound way. In my own work, I see many things that need to be changed in relation to power. For example, I think it was important here in Boston to build a new relationship with the police, so that they could become part of the solution to the problems, overcoming a very repressive position. It is possible to carry out good preventive work and avoid the use of force."

Teny Goss believes there should be more people working in the streets and that community services should be better. If the schools and social services in the poor sectors of the city are in bad condition, it only brings more poverty and misery to the already difficult lives of young people. However, the authorities often forget their neediest citizens and invest little in the city's poor areas. "It is important to show these kids that life is beautiful and worth living," says Teny Goss. "Unfortunately, many of them do not have this view and believe they will die young. They live in the midst of violence, where life is worth little and the future seems of little concern. But to give them a different vision, words have to be followed by action and they have to be able to see that their efforts to change are recognized in some way."

A group of churches in Cambridge, across the Charles River from Boston, has also joined the Coalition. In 1992 this city, home to Harvard University and the Massachusetts Institute of Technology (MIT), experienced a wave of juvenile violence that led municipal officials to consider long-term work with young people to prevent crises and head off problems before they occur. The programme is known as Positive EDGE (Education, Direction, Guidance and Empowerment), and works out of city hall, with public funds and support from the local churches. It is headed by Edward Harris, a lay deacon of the Union Baptist Church in Cambridge, who is in charge of a team of eight street workers, men and women between 19 and 50 years old. After five years, Positive EDGE, which began as a pilot programme, is considered by city youth as a place to go to for any problem, knowing that there will always be someone there willing to listen to them.

"The young people we assist are a part of the solution to the problems taking place," stresses Harris. "Many of them want to share what they think, what they feel. That is why it is important to spend time talking with them. A good part of our work has to do with building relations and combining attitudes of leadership and direction with a behaviour that sets an example. We have to be able to listen to teenagers, to include them at the table whenever we discuss issues that have to do with their education, the use of their free time, family relations and the problems that affect them, like drug use."

Harris is convinced that the community should better use available resources to respond to the needs of young people. Like Teny Goss, he also believes that police enforcement policies regarding young people need to be revised. The police force must open its doors to a dialogue with the community about its role in crime prevention and the work with juvenile offenders. "The police need to feel they are a part of the community," Harris insists. "It is important that they also listen to what young people think of their work. And police brutality must end."

Positive EDGE mediates in conflict situations and organizes weekend retreats to restore trust between people and also confidence in society and its institutions. "It is essential to break the influence that drug traffickers have on young people," Harris insists. "It is good to be up-front with the young people and ask them, 'What do you get from using drugs?' It is also important to show them that it is possible to change."

In its work with children and teenagers, the Boston Ten Point Coalition, supported by the city's mayor, has encouraged the creation of after-school programmes in the churches. Teams of volunteers provide children and teenagers recreational activities, help them with their homework and offer support in personal and family problems. André John and Matthew Gibson are in charge of this programme at the Azusa Christian Community. André was born in the Four Corners neighbourhood, Matthew is a Harvard graduate. Besides recreation and help with schoolwork, the two have developed a series of art, handicrafts and literary workshops, in which children and teenagers participate enthusiastically. On Friday evenings they organize a special activity, which includes a large meal and a film. "This is a way of coming together, sharing a fun time and keeping the kids off the streets," says Matthew Gibson. "We stay until 11:00. The parents know that the kids are involved in healthy activities here, and are also protected. Unfortunately, the rate of drug addiction among the parents of these kids tends to be very high, which makes it a delicate and none too easy task to discuss the dangers of smoking, alcoholism and drug addiction with them."

The Boston Ten Point Coalition also sponsors exchange programmes between youth leaders and their peers in other nearby cities, providing opportunities for networking and participation in education and training. It is working with one of its partners, the Emmanuel Gospel Center, on a project to locate twenty young ministers in churches throughout the city for a five-year period in order to develop a specific ministry for youth.

In the neighbourhoods of Roxbury and South Boston, a work training programme has been started to help youth who have finished their high school studies to obtain well-paid jobs. All these efforts provide support and give hope for the future.

Risk also touches families

In 1995 the state of Massachusetts domestic violence emergency hotline received 95,000 telephone calls, and 4000 women and children were received in emergency shelters. In Boston the police department responded to 13,000 incidents of domestic violence and made 3500 arrests for violations of restraining orders. A study by the state's probation department estimates that 43,000 children are exposed to violence in the home each year.

Because domestic violence is often critical in the inner cities, the Boston Ten Point Coalition joined with several other institutions to organize training activities for ministers on domestic violence. Through a series of seminars and workshops, supported financially by the police department, the ministers received information on the subject and discussed appropriate pastoral actions. Emphasis was placed on violence against women and on the impact of domestic violence on children. The ministers were advised on how to respond under different circumstances – when to offer pastoral care, when to report a case to the police, when to receive women and children in an emergency shelter, where to find protection in cases of severe or sustained violence.

The coalition also works specifically on preventing violence against children and on pastoral care for children who have witnessed violence in their homes. For this, it keeps in touch with the Child Witness to Violence Project of the Boston Medical Center. A study of 115 mothers by the pediatrics department of Boston Hospital disclosed that one of every ten children in these families had witnessed an attack with firearms or knives before the age of 6 – half in their homes, half in the community.

Aimee Thompson, the programme's community outreach coordinator, is in charge of a ten-week activity project for children affected by violence. "Although children may not have been the direct victims of violence," she says, "they are also victims simply for having witnessed it. The community must become aware of what is happening in homes and on the streets. With its help, women and children could overcome the isolation they are subject to in situations of domestic violence. We must create safe places where people can feel comfortable in sharing their situation. In addition, I believe there is a close connection between family violence and youth violence on the streets. Preventing violence at home means preventing problems that could arise later on, when the children who have witnessed this violence reach adolescence."

The project identifies children who have witnessed violence, supports them so that they are able to overcome the trauma, and provides counseling for families, teachers and volunteers from churches and public service organizations that work with children. "Intervention in these cases must be quick," according to Aimee Thompson. "Treatment in general takes place in the child's own environment. We work with the family, and particularly with the school, so that they are able to help the child overcome the trauma. We also provide psychological treatment whenever necessary, using therapeutic games. Children who have been victims of violence are referred to other services."

Another aspect of preventing violence which concerns African American churches in Boston has to do with fatherhood. As noted earlier, fewer than 30 percent of inner-city African American homes have a stable adult male presence. There are many reasons why men abandon their families and avoid taking care of them. Most are related to social and cultural issues and to male participation in the criminal world.

The Boston Ten Point Coalition has carried out activities to strengthen men's participation in their families and their relationships with their children. Plans have been made with the Department of Revenue and the Child Enforcement Services to carry out programmes to help fathers relate with their children. Eugene Rivers and Mark Scott, his assistant at the Azusa Community, offer a series of fatherhood workshops as part of their prison ministry at the correctional institution in Concord, where they work with 120 inmates through four-week activity cycles. "Inmate response is good," points out Mark Scott. "We see them attending on a regular basis, participating in the discussions and beginning to feel the need to change their behaviour."

The ministers saw the importance of dealing with the issue of fatherhood since most of the inmates already had small children. They felt it would be good to help them to think about their role as parents, the expectations of their spouses and children and their responsibility towards their families and society. "It is essential to work with the inmates before they are back on the street," says Eugene Rivers. "Life in prison is very hard, and we know that without proper guidance and counselling they could be facing new difficulties upon returning to their homes and neighbourhood." The effective presence of the churches in this task can make an important difference in the former inmates' return to their families.

Preventing violence and community relations

Changes in Boston's social makeup have been quick and profound. Although the population has remained around 570,000, half of the city's residents moved out during the 1980s and were replaced by new neighbours. Of the new residents between 1985 and 1990, one in four belonged to a new immigrant group in the United States. For this reason, many people feel that Boston has become a city where most of the residents do not know each other. Urban experts believe that it is beneficial for a city's population to be renewed, but if the annual population turnover exceeds 5 percent a year (the figure for Boston in recent years has been twice that), serious problems can result. A large percentage of the new residents may find it difficult to know and assimilate the values and norms of behaviour, thus weakening the social fabric.

Typical of this turnover is the Codman Square neighbourhood in Dorchester. Towards the end of the 1970s, it was the scene of many violent racial incidents. Slowly businesses began to begin to close their doors and people moved out. Latin, Cambodian and Vietnamese immigrants moved in, changing the face of what had been a predominantly African American neighbourhood. In 1979, the community decided to open the Codman Square Health Center to animate community relations. Within several years the centre was facilitating a whole range of activities fostering community integration. A community centre now operates out of its previous offices, and an abandoned building across the street was equipped with the modern facilities it needed to provide health care.

Several member churches of the Boston Ten Point Coalition are supporting the violence prevention and community development programmes promoted there. "How do you teach people not to be violent?" asks director Bill Walczak. He views violence as the language of those who have no other means to express themselves. "Problems are resolved in the measure to which the community begins to work together. That is why we decided to make this health centre a place open to the community, with emphasis on prevention. We opened up spaces here for people to meet, talk and celebrate."

About 40 of the centre's staff members have received special training in preventing violence, detecting cases of domestic violence and supporting victims in their recovery. The centre has developed a formation programme for community health workers, who can also assist in developing crime watchers and a Violence Prevention Task Force. The underlying idea is that no citizen should have to experience violence. Attention has also been given to violence in high schools, leading to prevention efforts involving parents, students and teachers. "We are interested in the centre having a holistic understanding of health," says Bill Walczak. "We want to improve the quality of life of the people in all its aspects, and for this we link up with all community entities and organizations within our sphere of action. Unfortunately, there are not enough public funds for actions of a larger scope, but we do what we can to reach all of the people that surround us."

The Codman Square Health Center now carries out 100,000 consultations a year besides its work in the community centre, which houses a youth centre, an educational and work training support centre, counselling for parents, a club for grandparents who are rearing their grandchildren, a drop-in centre for informal activities and a meeting hall for community and cultural events and special programmes. As the neighbourhood's social fabric begins to be restored, businesses are gradually coming back and neighbours are involved in keeping it clean. The face of Codman Square is changing once more, becoming a habitable place able to shelter working families and neighbours interested in community.

The Boston Ten Point Coalition is also taking part with the Boston Police Department, the probation office, the Department of Youth Services, the justice system and the Boston Community Centers in Operation Ceasefire, an effort to prevent young people from falling into crime by intervening when a person first has problems with the authorities and by supporting the workings of the justice system when young people do break the law. For this work, the Coalition received special recognition from the Boston Police Department.

In March 1998, a Boston police official met with a group of ministers of the Boston Ten Point Coalition who were concerned about the growing influence on city youth from two well-known west coast gangs, the Crips and the Bloods. The officer warned the ministers of the dangers that hundreds of young people would face if these gangs, noted for their street riots and violence, were able to penetrate into the city. In addition, he asked the ministers' help in beginning an immediate preventive task.

The fear was that these new gangs, in an effort to gain supporters in eastern cities, would take the place of Boston gangs that had disappeared after 1992, when the street prevention and monitoring work had been most intense. West coast gangs are not only involved in drug trafficking and use but also in arms sales. Because of variations in state laws within the US, it is fairly easy to buy weapons in the southern states and sell them on the black market at a much higher price in the north, where the sale of firearms to minors is more closely regulated. For example, a semi-automatic rifle purchased in Florida for $300 may be sold in the north for almost $1000.

In view of this danger, the ministers and the police developed a plan to visit schools and the homes of young people suspected of being in contact with these gangs. The proposal received immediate support from Cardinal Law. The task was coordinated by Jeffrey Brown, pastor of Union Baptist Church in Cambridge and a founder of the Coalition, and Prince Woodberry, pastor of Grace Church of All Nations in Dorchester. Both the ministers and the police officers advised the young people of the danger of becoming involved with these gangs and warned that the city would not tolerate a resurgence of violence. The preventive task was not limited to the African American community. Although in Los Angeles, most of the Crips and Bloods are African American, the racial groups in Boston are mixed, with a high presence of Hispanics, Asians, whites and African Americans in the gangs. Moreover, unlike most other cities, gang territories are less fixed in Boston, and members can come from any neighbourhood. Thus it was important to cover the entire city in this preventive task.

Counteracting violence also involves the courts. In Dorchester, probation officer Bernard Fitzgerald knows that the ministers and churches are collaborating in the search for alternatives that can take young people out of the cycle of violence. About 800 young people between 17 and 25 are under the probation system in this district. To prepare them for a better future, they are given compulsory reading and discussion classes on subjects that call on them to be responsible citizens, while at the same time doing community service under the supervision and guidance of different institutions, among them the churches. "I think there are many young people going through situations that make them vulnerable," Fitzgerald points out. "We try to make sure that what they receive through the probation system will make a difference in their lives and allow them to follow a better path, away from violence."

The work carried out by Rev. Clovis Turner and a group of helpers in the women's correctional facility in Framingham Hill also aims at overcoming violence. A member of the pastoral team of the Grace for All Nations church in Dorchester, Clovis Turner visits this prison, with more than 600 female inmates, weekly, believing it is important for the inmates to count on the regular presence of the churches. "The inmates trust the group that comes from the church, because they know their dedication. They know we will be with them each week and that we never fail when we organize an activity. This is very important, because it creates a climate of trust and at the same time gives security to the women, who beyond their delinquent conduct have suffered a lot." The work with the inmates upon their release involves providing constant support, so that their re-insertion into society and re-encounter with their families is as little traumatic as possible.

The leaders of the Boston Ten Point Coalition know the critical importance of ending violence in the city streets in order to open up the way for progress and development in the neighbourhoods. But they also know that achieving this requires the joint efforts of the authorities, the business community and neighbours. "If we have peace, there will be jobs," points out Jeffrey Brown. "But also if there are no jobs, there will be no peace. Our responsibility also involves bringing resources to the neighbourhoods. Otherwise, it will be very difficult to offer new opportunities to young people."

6. Durban

The Good Friday worship service was highly charged with emotion. A few weeks earlier, sectarian violence had rocked Bhambayi, a settlement on the outskirts of Durban, in the province of Kwazulu Natal, South Africa. Many people had lost their lives, homes were burned, property was destroyed. The confrontations had eventually ceased thanks to an appeal from the churches, the political parties involved in the dispute, the authorities and the people. Now, in this service, peace was being celebrated. The Good Friday procession down the main aisle of Durban's Roman Catholic cathedral was led by a cross made of charred wood from the burned houses of two Bhambayi families from opposing parties who had lost all their belongings during the dispute. Later in the service, people placed flowers on the cross to symbolize the new life with peace that everyone was longing for.

After the service, the cross was taken to Bhambayi and placed next to the stream crossing the settlement which the opposing groups used to mark their territorial boundary. Every day, people could be seen approaching the cross to pray. One day, a woman stopped to pray, as was her custom. From the other side of the stream, someone saw in her a perfect target on which to vent his hatred. He shot. The woman dropped dead at the foot of the cross. Hours later, a group of local people took the cross down from the place where it had been put with so much hope.

Political confrontations in Kwazulu Natal, a province of 8 million people, have killed 11,600 and injured more than 30,000 over the past decade. Hundreds of properties have been destroyed – private homes, businesses, community centres, schools and clinics. There are half a million displaced people in the province.

The high degree of political intolerance, particularly at the community level, has created numerous "no-go areas", in which members of one political party or the other put their lives at risk if they dare to enter. So it is that supermarkets, schools, clinics and even public water sources find themselves in places where part of the population does not in effect have access to them. This of course aggravates the already precarious living conditions in the townships, settlements and shantytowns, increasing the social tensions further.

The political struggle in Kwazulu Natal began in the early 1980s, and grew in the townships and settlements around Durban until it exploded violently in 1985. Some have compared it to an undeclared war, with peaks of violence in 1987 and 1990. The number of victims has been high, but since 1994 the democratic process and the end of apartheid have made it possible to work more intensively for peace in the communities. Violence continues to the present, though at a steadily reduced number of flashpoints.

The high level of violence in Kwazulu Natal is rooted in the power struggle between the Inkatha Freedom Party (IFP) and the African National Congress (ANC). The rivalry deepened in 1990, when the government lifted the ban against the ANC and negotiations for a non-racial constitution began. Those familiar with the conflict identify several political factors that feed the violence:

- A "culture of violence" has developed in the region, exacerbated by the warrior tradition of the Zulus and the territorial struggles that have been endemic for many generations in certain areas. Weapons are readily available and effective police controls are lacking. When violence breaks out, it is often impossible to determine whether it is a fight between clans or between numbers of different parties.
- Increased political activity has led to the mobilization of the population, and the practice of political patronage has strengthened the identification of people with one party or the other.
- Verbal confrontations between national or provincial leaders of the IFP and ANC, as well as accusations that the IFP collaborated with the former white minority apartheid regime, have fuelled the tensions.

Environmental and social conditions make things worse. Nearly 37 percent of the population lives in informal settlements or shantytowns – an unplanned urbanization in which basic services are virtually nonexistent. Thousands of families live without electricity, water, sewers, roads, health centres or schools. Families crowd into one or two rooms in houses made of metal, wood or plastic sheeting. The rapid urbanization and the fact that the people come from different parts of the province mean that the residents lack a common history, which makes it difficult to build the community spirit which could overcome the bitter competition over scarce resources in overpopulated areas.

Without community ties, people look elsewhere for a new sense of belonging. As a result, some identify fanatically with a political party, others join the gangs that attempt to control the rest of the population. Added to this are unemployment rates of almost 25 percent of the economically active population, and 46 percent among people under 25. The incidence is much higher among the black population. And since the people have not yet seen their expectations of a better life fulfilled under a democratic government, they are less and less willing to continue to tolerate these conditions.

Another legacy of the apartheid era is the intervention of "third forces" in conflicts. These are usually made up of former members of the racist security forces who seek to exercise a destabilizing influence against the new South African democracy.

Work for peace in Kwazulu Natal has only been possible thanks to the profound constitutional and legislative changes that have taken place since 1994 at the national, provincial and local levels. It involves many sectors of society – grassroots groups, community and non-governmental organizations, churches and religious associations, business, political and religious leaders – which have been willing to work together from different angles to overcome the destruction left by political violence in the region.

Churches work for justice and peace

In 1976, the social, political and human rights situation in South Africa challenged the churches in Kwazulu Natal to begin working in a new way. There were many demands for the churches to organize actions in the area of social justice, but the Natal Council of Churches had no staff at the time. So the churches decided to form a new organization, under the name Diakonia, to advise and assist them in their service and defence of human rights. In 1994, based on the experience garnered from the joint work of the churches, the Diakonia Council of Churches (DCC) was formed, with a membership of sixteen Protestant, Evangelical, Catholic and Orthodox churches and three ecumenical organizations. Its headquarters are in Durban, South Africa's second largest city and the largest port in southern Africa. The city's location on the Indian Ocean makes it an important centre for economic development with good prospects for the future.

"Three big issues challenged us as we started this organization in 1976," recalls DCC director Paddy Kearney. "There were the arbitrary detentions and torture, often causing the death of those under arrest; the housing problems affecting over half the population; and the apartheid laws, which imposed the forced removal of the population from one area to another. Our first public act was a funeral for Joseph Mdluli, a prisoner who had died in jail, victim to the torture and ill treatment he received. About a thousand people attended the funeral, and this caused us many problems with the security police, as well as tensions with the congregations, including the accusation that we were communists."

Responding to violence has characterized the work of Diakonia almost from the beginning. A school boycott in 1980 evoked brutal repression against the students. Paddy Kearney recalls that at the time "some ministers abandoned their congregations, whereas others stood firm in a non-partisan position, attempting to mediate in conflicts with courage and valour. The burning down of property was used as a political weapon. Often these attacks were carried out with collaboration from the police, who provided logistical support, information and weapons. Ignorance, poverty and the lack of education made the people easy targets of political propaganda. Political leaders were largely responsible for what happened at that time. In the churches, we worked in situations of real danger, even risking the lives of the mediators."

Diakonia became a member of the United Democratic Front (UDF), an umbrella body made up of some 600 non-governmental organizations. Later it changed its membership to the category of observer when the UDF's work became linked to the political struggle. With the political opening that came at the beginning of the 1990s, when the ANC was legalized and Nelson Mandela and other top leaders freed, Diakonia began to work on education for multi-party democracy, inviting representatives from all political parties to present their ideas and proposals. In 1992, this work began to concentrate on the electoral process, helping people to register to vote and teaching them to participate actively in the entire process, discussing the different platforms and getting to know the candidates.

As the political confrontations intensified between the IFP and the UDF, which later became a part of the ANC, Diakonia received more and more requests to intervene in these conflicts, which were causing countless victims each day. People had to flee their homes, which were burned down by their political opponents, and start over in the suburbs, townships and settlements.

Today the DCC has five main programmes, of which four are directly related to work for peace in Kwazulu Natal.(1) The first involves concrete engagement in the peace processes going on in the cities, townships, settlements and shantytowns, as well as in the rural areas. (2) A second programmatic emphasis is education for democracy. Because the periods prior to elections tend to be more violent, special efforts are made to develop in the people a multi-party and pluralist vision of South African democracy. (3) Work for economic justice is basic to achieving social peace. The DCC sponsors training in life skills, technical skills and business management for hundreds of unemployed people. (4) DCC also carries out advisory work for community development through a network of 12 resource centres where people can get legal aid regarding unemployment, pension and disability benefits, workers' compensation and accident insurance claims. These centres also lobby at the local legislative level to obtain benefits for the community. Because of the credibility of their work and the trust people have in them, staff from these centres have also been trained as statement-takers for South Africa's Truth and Reconciliation Commission (TRC). (5) The fifth area of work is the fight against AIDS in Kwazulu Natal, which has claimed 150,000 lives since 1991. The DCC seeks to raise awareness of this crisis with the population at large and encourages its member churches to care for persons living with AIDS and the thousands of children orphaned by the loss of their parents to this disease.

The DCC is also active in the World Conference on Religion and Peace (WCRP), which has a chapter in Durban. Among the people of Kwazulu Natal, especially the Durban Functional Region, are followers of all the major world religions. Many decades ago the largest Indian population outside of India settled in this region. Mahatma Gandhi lived here, and his granddaughter Ela Gandhi is currently an ANC member of parliament. Hindus, Muslims, Jews, Buddhists and Christians have places of worship in the region and carry out cultural and religious activities in a climate of broad pluralism.

"Our work began in the early 1980s, with the nonviolence movement, calling on people of all faiths to work for justice and peace," recalls Susan Brittion, co-moderator of the WCRP chapter in Durban. "We were able to work with people from all the religious confessions represented in the city, with important campaigns such as the ones to put an end to racism on the beaches and to halt obligatory conscription by the security forces. We did this convinced that people of faith must be independent in developing work on behalf of the entire population." The section of the Bill of Rights of the new South African constitution dealing with religious rights and responsibilities reflects proposals made by the WCRP.

A recent campaign in Durban took as its theme "Celebration of the Right to Be". There were exhibits, panel discussions and activities for children in the context of a broad debate on tolerance, peace and justice in relations between people of different cultural, religious and racial origins. At the national level, the WCRP has provided support for the Truth and Reconciliation Commission, and its president, attorney Yasmine Sooka, is a member of the TRC. Religious leaders of all faiths took part in a ceremony at Durban city hall to launch the TRC's work – a concrete testimony to the desire to protect and respect the religious and cultural rights of all South Africans.

As part of its work for dialogue and tolerance between the different religious groups, the WCRP sponsors the Desmond Tutu Annual Peace Lecture in Durban; recent guests have included the Dalai Lama and Indian feminist Vandana Shiva.

Challenges for peace in Bhambayi

The Gandhi family property was located in Inanda, in a rural area on the outskirts of Durban. Originally, the apartheid government had not assigned this area to any ethnic group, and whites, Indians and blacks all had farms there, growing sugar cane, vegetables and fruits. Over time, the land was leased to new families pushed out of the cities by the apartheid policies. Gradually, this led to divisions and mistrust among the population. In the mid-1980s the government tried to buy the lands of the Indian families. They refused to sell, and the Department of Cooperation and Development told the black population that no development projects would be carried out in the area as long as Indians were living there. Ela Gandhi and her husband, who had been living on Sarvodaya, a property which had belonged to Mahatma Gandhi, were detained.

Anger over the government's announcement disturbed relations between the racial groups. Within a few weeks, a climate of violence developed, provoked by what many saw as the intervention of "third forces" in the area. Unrestrained violence began in August 1985, when angry groups set fire for the first time to businesses belonging to Indian families near the police station in Inanda. Arson, beatings and killings continued for five days. Some entire families disappeared; others lost all their belongings and had to flee to Phoenix, a nearby township occupied by Indian families. The Gandhi home was completely destroyed – the walls torn down, the floors ripped up and the roof tiles taken away. Later, other families invaded the New Farm lands next to Inanda, which belonged to 44 black farm families who had fled in fear for their lives.

Mew Ramgobin, chair of the Phoenix Settlement Trust, later told the TRC that the riots in which the Gandhi settlement was destroyed took place with the knowledge of the security forces and were part of a plan to enforce apartheid policies in the area. What the authorities at that time described as "confrontations between Indians and Africans" were in fact brought about by a policy of ethnic cleansing. By refusing to sell their lands to the government, the Indian owners were hindering its plans to create a Kwazulu bantustan in the area. When Mew Ramgobin, who represented the Indian community in the negotiations with the Department of Cooperation and Development at that time, asked the security forces to protect the people and their property, they instead conspired with the people who were looting and setting fire to properties in Inanda and later attacked Phoenix.

At first the black people who took over the place, which was given the name Bhambayi (Bombay), were dominated by the IFP. In 1989, however, the UDF gained control after a series of riots, deaths and the burning of houses. IFP members returned in 1993, and the conflict began anew, with a peak in communal violence that took the lives of about a thousand people, including women and children, and the destruction of dozens of homes. After these very serious events, the Kwazulu Natal Regional Peace Committee (on which the DCC is now represented) intervened.

The work for peace in South Africa grew out of far-reaching political agreements in preparation for the 1994 elections which would mark the end of apartheid and establish multi-party democracy. The National Peace Accord signed by the South African political parties in November 1991 was intended to prevent the buildup of confrontations and violence during the pre-electoral period. It also provided for the training of monitors to mediate and intervene in conflicts so that the political demonstrations and marches could be peaceful. A code of conduct was established for the political parties and security forces, with guidelines to encourage development and socio-economic reconstruction. The Goldstone Commission was created to prevent and publicly denounce violence and intimidation; and structures were established to resolve conflicts and to ensure broad public participation in creating a climate of tolerance in conflict situations.

The Kwazulu Natal Regional Peace Committee decided that its work should focus on the efforts of local leadership, the problems of displaced people and the role of the police in instigating violence and violating human rights. It established local peace committees made up of representatives from two other committees: one on security and the other on development. This ensured community participation in detecting problems, taking initiatives to avoid conflicts, facilitating development and reconstruction and supporting relocation of displaced families. Soon 250 local peace committees had been set up in the province, with the participation of 7000 voluntary peace workers, representatives of civil society, political parties, government and security institutions.

In Bhambayi the local committee began to search for solutions to the serious division that had led to the violence in the area. As a first step, the former inhabitants of New Farm, a few of whom have returned to this area, decided to donate a piece of land in the centre of Bhambayi for a community centre. "The donation of this land was our way of contributing to peace," says Meshack Ndlorn. "The site is right in the middle of this settlement, and we feel that the existence of a community centre here helps to build lasting ties between the people and also creates confidence in the possibility of working together. It is important that we be united in making decisions, since we need to think about the future of this settlement." The Durban Metropolitan Council decided to donate the building, recognizing the community for having initiated a peace process and understanding that people must begin to enjoy the fruits of peace if they are to be convinced not to return to violence.

Bongani Mbatha, who chairs the Bhambayi reconstruction and development committee, says that "if the people do not unite, we will not be successful in developing our community or in doing constructive things. There were a series of priorities for us in Bhambayi: public lighting in the street, provision of potable water and roads and construction of a bridge over the stream at the entrance to the settlement. We decided that the bridge and roads would be our first task, as well as installing several public taps for potable water. The workers would all come from our settlement. We kept in mind a party balance in selecting the workers and accepted having outside supervisors to train the workers. Thus, in the future our workers would be able to take care of any necessary repairs."

Before the work began, an agreement was signed with the Phoenix Settlement Trust for the ownership of the land. The Durban Metropolitan Council freed 90 percent of the Gandhi property, retaining the rest to rebuild the house and set up a museum, library and post office, as well as the clinic and printing press that were there before the arson attacks.

"We do not gain anything from violence," says Bongani Mbatha. "No one can say he or she wins from violence. On the other hand, if we begin a peace process, we all win. There is still much to be done in Bhambayi, but the development accomplished so far is appreciated by all. We have our homes, potable water and electricity. And we have also learned to negotiate without conflicts. But the work for peace must flow from the heart. In addition, only with peace will we be able to build democracy. For me, living in democracy means going to sleep at night without fear, trusting my neighbours and defending life."

The key role of peace monitors

The Vuleka Trust, an ecumenical organization of the Anglican, Methodist and Catholic churches, operates the Koinonia Conference Centre, located in the Valley of a Thousand Hills, a rural area close to Durban. Rev. Athol Jennings was the director of this centre from 1984 to 1998. A pioneer in mediation work in Kwazulu Natal, he was awarded the Martin Luther King Jr Prize by the US Peace Institute for his contribution to nonviolent conflict resolution.

Recognizing that conflict resolution would be critical for the future of South Africa, Athol Jennings started a course to train peace monitors which nearly 2000 people have followed since 1990. The Vuleka Trust coordinated most of the programmes of the Ecumenical Peace Making Process and has trained persons from local churches involved in the continuous monitoring of their communities. It has also specialized in the training of trainers, so that peace work skills could be spread throughout the entire province. "Achieving democracy in South Africa in a climate of peace and understanding is truly a miracle," Athol Jennings says.

The training courses begin with a module on "Basic Human Relations", aimed at developing essential skills for interpersonal relationships. The second module introduces "Effective Negotiation Skills", and the third, "Mediation Skills", explains the ins and outs of conflicts for those who are about to enter into a negotiation process. A fourth module, "Handling Conflict Creatively", explains how conflict can be transformed by allowing two processes to develop: (1) moving from individual to community interests and needs, thus restoring holistic relations and healing wounds; (2) moving from structures that reinforce divisions to those which develop inclusive communities through work for justice, reconciliation and peace.

During 1997, there were 20 training workshops in Zulu and English at the Koinonia Conference Centre with people from both urban and rural areas. René Daries, who trains peace monitors, notes that "we have always tried to customize the working materials for peace, so that they relate to the South African context. We work in inter-disciplinary teams, and the monitors who finish the courses have a professional profile that is very respected by the communities."

Among those communities where peace monitors trained by the Vuleka Trust are working is Bhambayi. One of the provisions of the basic agreement reached by the opposing political parties in this settlement in 1993 was that ten members from each party should be trained as peace monitors and recognized as such by the community. "Our task is to promote peace in personal and community relations and also to treat criminals as such," affirms Stanley Bulose, who is supervisor of the peace monitors in Bhambayi. He insists that the community must not shelter those who commit criminal acts, regardless of their political affiliation.

Despite the agreement which designated them, the peace monitors did suffer attacks at the outset; and one of them, Johnson Nkambi, was killed in the line of duty. Because the monitors were not willing to turn a blind eye to any kind of criminality, some people in the community believed they were police informers. But little by little, the people began to understand their true role; and their presence eventually led to a substantial reduction of violence and delinquency. Their irreproachable behaviour has earned them the support of local leaders, who have themselves become good negotiators in resolving conflicts.

At first the peace monitors were on 24-hour call in the community; now they work only during the day. Francis Armitage, a white man who was the first peace monitor in Bhambayi, was supported by the Diakonia Council of Churches. He had to fulfill a high-risk task, not only mediating in conflicts between the people but also monitoring police actions. Often Armitage went out on patrol with police to make sure they were fulfilling their duties with justice and impartiality. Few police officers at the time were black, and both white and Indian officers often acted in a discriminatory and prejudiced manner, harassing the people and creating even more tension. Today, most of the police in the Bhambayi area are black, and police-community relations have greatly improved.

Political leaders often come to the monitors when they want to meet, even asking them to chair meetings and organize the agenda. This level of trust results in part from the fact that the peace monitors have been selected by their community, as well as their constant patrolling which allows them to get to know each family and to become aware of problems as they arise.

"A typical work day for a peace monitor involves patrolling the streets, working with the people to give them trust and collaborating in all of the community's development tasks," according to Stanley Bulose. "We work a lot on educating the community about how to resolve conflicts without fighting. On weekends we often organize workshops to share our work. I think we have accomplished much in our community during these years. People now know there will be development if there is peace. When we built the bridge at the entrance to the settlement, we made sure that the workers came from both parties, so they could get to know and trust each other. In this way they would be able to overcome prejudices more easily."

Peace monitor Themba Sokhulu, a member of the Network of Independent Monitors who work with the Ecumenical Monitoring Programme in South Africa, has done extensive research into the causes of violence, concluding that it is often encouraged by "third forces", including the private armies of political leaders, and by former police officers. "It is important for us also to monitor the police and encourage and educate residents to be a part of the community police forums," Themba Sokhulu says. "It is also good to monitor the private security companies. Many of them are owned by former members of the security forces, and have elements in their ranks with a racist background."

Some delinquent bands involved in the arms and drug trade are also made up of former members of the security forces. While South African law permits bearing arms for personal safety, there is a vast black market in weapons ranging from automatic rifles like the Russian AK-47 to grenades, mortars, anti-tank mines and explosives. In 1996, 45 percent of all illegal weapons confiscated by South African police were found in Kwazulu Natal.

Testimony before the TRC has revealed how the apartheid regime exploited the existing political animosities in Kwazulu Natal between the ANC and the IFP to provoke violence by each group against the other. Much of the current insecurity in the province stems from this orientation of the police forces to political destabilization rather than prevention and investigation of crime. Moreover, the political violence in this region provided a smokescreen to hide the activities of organized crime. The investigative monitoring of persons like Themba Sokhulu provides organizations such as the Diakonia Council of Churches with up-to-date information on the development of violent events and their motives, enabling them to plan actions and training based on this knowledge.

Many other church leaders have been recognized by the communities for their important contributions to peace at the grassroots level. One is Miriam Celle, who worked for peace in Bhambayi during one of the most violent periods there and who has also received the Martin Luther King Prize. "There is nothing left to do unless the church has an active presence in the place," says this Methodist woman, who joined with members from other churches to organize prayer meetings in Bhambayi so that the violence would cease. "On one occasion, our lives were miraculously saved. We were holding a prayer meeting, when a shooting took place between opposing bands and we were left in the middle of the standoff. However, we continued to pray. The shooting stopped and no one was wounded.

"We would meet to pray wearing our different church uniforms. Almost all of us were women, because the men were afraid of losing their lives if they joined us. We decided to speak with the women first, because we knew that even though they did not fight, they often instigated men to violence. Those were very dramatic times."

Finally, the group led by Miriam Celle was able to hold a mass worship service in Bhambayi, with 800 people from different denominations. Many residents confessed their guilt, wishing to free their spirits from so much violence. There were many tears and prayers and the people left the service encouraged to work for peace. To symbolize a new stage in the relations between the people, a festive celebration was organized.

There are now no longer boundaries between communities in Bhambayi. People can walk freely in the streets, and the results of development made possible by peaceful coexistence are gradually becoming visible. The people proudly point out the bridge built with everyone's help, as well as the roads and potable water taps. They are now waiting for the Durban Metropolitan Council to implement a project that will allow the complete reconstruction of the area and better living conditions for all.

Involving young people in peace-building

Workshops at the Koinonia Conference Centre and in the townships encourage the active participation of young people in their communities and the recognition of youth leadership in development and work for democracy. For example, a workshop in 1996 brought together school principals, teachers and students from the Phoenix area, where Bhambayi is located, to examine the challenges posed by racial integration. In addition, 80 ninth grade students worked on subjects like the building of trust, human relations and teamwork.

Boy Mzimela, a peace monitor for the Independent Projects Trust, underscores the value of work with young people in the schools, which were long considered the territory of one or another political party. "When you work with young people, it is important to see what they can do together. It is good to train them outside their normal environment, so that they do not feel intimidated by the negative forces that constantly bear down on them," he observes. "It has been very difficult to stop the violence in the schools, since many students were combatants during the period prior to democracy and were very old and experienced for their age. They grew up in gangs and also in the arms and drug trade. Schools were unsafe places, and even today there are problems in some of the schools in the settlements. There are frequent acts of vandalism and often school furniture ends up in the informal settlements."

Boy Mzimela feels that parents as well as principals, teachers and students should be included in conflict resolution. With training, he believes, the school community can establish its own code of discipline. It is important to encourage a climate of coexistence, oriented to learning, tolerance and better communication among different racial and political groups.

In Bhambayi, where 80 percent of the population is under 30, the community selected five young people to lead the youth participation in the political and socioeconomic development of the area. One of them, Sithembiso Zulu, identifies the critical role of youth groups in providing civic education to encourage peaceful coexistence. It is also important to train workers for the development of the area. Young people participated in building the bridge at the entrance to the settlement and the community centre. "We have advanced a lot over the last few years, but there is still much to be done," Sithembiso Zulu admits. "The lack of education and work training create problems of violence. We still have not been able to respond to the daily needs of the people, and it is important to do so. People are willing to help. The community is tired of conflicts and is more interested in moving ahead than in fighting."

Jabulani Lubinyane, a young IFP leader, explains why his party supported the idea of training local peace monitors. "The people here are better able to understand the situation," he says. "We accept the work of outside peace monitors, but they come and go. We are interested in having local peace monitors because only they can fully understand the nature of the violence here. We young people have learned a lot from these monitors. They speak to us frankly about the consequences of violence. They make us see the problems of those who suffer traumas from the fighting, and encourage us to become involved in the development of the community."

One of the serious problems for local youth, regardless of political affiliation, is the lack of jobs. Most of them married as adolescents and have their own families to take care of. Although many have received work training, they cannot find a job and this is discouraging. Still, Jabulani Lubinyane says, the young people do not want to leave Bhambayi. "We want to stay here, because there is no longer violence and we have nothing to fear. We feel our future is in this place."

The DCC is also working with the Kwazulu Natal Violence Survivor Programme, part of which is aimed at children who have experienced physical violence or sexual abuse in their homes or in the community. About 25 children from Bhambayi go each week to Durban for therapeutic treatment. Mothers also receive help, and there is counselling and treatment available for battered women. In addition, work is carried out in the community itself, with cooking and sewing workshops for women and a crèche for the children. Miriam Celle is also carrying out a significant work with victims of violence in

Bhambayi, focusing on abandoned children, street children and women.

Mike Vorster, manager of the DCC Peace Committee, and Mbonambi Khuzwayo, organizer of the DCC Peace Process programme, believe that much has been accomplished in Bhambayi over the past few years. The peace process initiated between the different political parties was accompanied by development initiatives which in turn encouraged the peace talks. The population is now convinced that it is worthwhile to live in peace and this allows for progress. The churches have been present in all this, accompanying the leadership, encouraging people's spirituality and supporting young people, women and adults in improving their living conditions. Although much remains to be done, the bridge at the entrance to Bhambayi is a symbol of the unity of the community. Together, they were able to build it, and together now they must ensure the realization of other aspirations for development.

After the sad episode of the cross placed by the stream after the Good Friday worship service, other crosses have been placed in the neighbourhood and continue to stand as witnesses to the peace achieved. The adults see dialogue and peaceful coexistence as possible, although they are concerned that their children still do not play together. Surely the challenge for Bhambayi, as for many other similar communities in South Africa and elsewhere, is to continue working for peace until the children are able to play together without fear.

7. Suva

"I do not want to become a museum piece." Taniela Tabu, a Methodist lay person and political leader of the Fijian Christian Fellowship Party, is fearful that Fiji's new constitution "opens the way for us indigenous Fijians soon to be overcome by foreigners. We are completely exposed. Our race could disappear within 200 years. Foreigners would take over the political power and our descendants would then be left without land. There are still many citizens who are not aware of this threat."

These dramatic words express a fear that many indigenous Fijians share: that of losing political control in their country. Taniela Tabu believes that the interests of indigenous Fijians were better protected under the constitution established after a nationalist military coup in 1990.

Living in a harmonious multi-cultural and multi-racial society, meeting the demands of all for equal political, economic, social and cultural rights, is a challenge that takes on particular dimensions in Fiji. The South Pacific island nation has a population of 770,000, of whom 51.1 percent are indigenous Fijians, 96 percent of them Christian, and 43.6 percent are Indo-Fijian, most of them Hindus, although 8 percent are also Sikhs, Muslims, Christians and there are smaller numbers of Buddhists and Baha'is. The rest of the population is of Chinese or European origin, or come from other Pacific islands. A special case is that of the small (43 sq. km.) island of Rotuma, which was annexed to Fiji during the colonial period. Of the 8000 Rotumans, only 2500 continue to live on their original island. While they are racially and culturally more akin to the people of Tonga and Samoa, they are accepted by Fijians without much difficulty.

The roots of the situation which now makes many indigenous Fijians fearful lie in the century of British colonial rule, when segregation between the different racial groups was socially accepted. The 330 islands of the Fiji archipelago formally became a British colony in 1874. The British brought in Indian labourers to work on the sugar cane plantations, initially as temporary residents who thus had little contact with the indigenous Fijians and Europeans. But as time passed, it became evident that the Indian population was there to stay. Mutual mistrust began to emerge, fostered by the colonial authorities in order to confirm their dominance over the people.

During the 1920s, a growing number of Indo-Fijians left the sugar cane plantations to become farmers or skilled workers. They also began to gain ground in the commercial sector, the professions and higher education. Little by little, the Indo-Fijian community began to organize itself and demand respect for its economic, social and political rights. The colonial authorities systematically opposed this, interpreting the protests as attempts to undermine the interests and rights of the indigenous Fijians. Major strikes by sugar workers in 1921 and 1943 and by sugar producers in 1943 and 1960 were repressed using indigenous Fijian forces and the power of the chiefs to influence the people against Indian demands. Thus, the concept of an "Indian threat" gained currency, allowing the white population and the government to divide the workers' movement, introduce racial segregation in the trade unions and nurture suspicion between the two main ethnic groups living on the islands. Even today, the main trade unions continue to be divided along racial lines.

Mistrust was fed by the strict ethnic separation, which meant that indigenous Fijians and the Indo-Fijians knew virtually nothing of each other. Fijians lived in their villages and had their own administration; Indians lived around the sugar cane plantations. The Suva Grammar School did not accept Fijians or Indians, though "part-European" students could be admitted if they met certain educational, economic and social qualifications. Even in the Sacred Heart cathedral, the different races were separated.

The churches' educational system also fostered segregation. At the beginning, most schools were run by Methodist or Catholic missions and attended by indigenous Fijian children, since it was this population which had accepted Christianity. When Indians began to set up their own schools at the turn of the century, it was not the intention to create segregated schools, but this is what in fact happened because of the geographical location and the language of instruction. During the 1930s educators from New Zealand took over control of education in Fiji, schools began to open up to the different races and English was imposed as the only language of instruction – an attempt to achieve a Westernized integration which took no account of the cultural and linguistic heritage of either people. Both accepted this, but only because they saw English as a vehicle for moving up socially and relating with the outside world. When Fiji declared its independence in 1970, 85 percent of the secondary schools had students of more than one race, a trend which continues – although in 42 percent of the schools 90 percent of the students are either Indian or Fijian.

In the run-up to the country's independence, two main political parties were formed along ethnic lines: the Alliance Party of indigenous Fijians and the Indian National Federation Party (NFP), formed by Indo-Fijians. There was discussion in the drafting of the constitution about how to maintain a balance of power and avoid ethnic conflict, but the British parliamentary model adopted was not able to respond to the expectations of equality between the races.

The political scene altered dramatically in 1987. A coalition between the NFP and the recently created Labour Party, headed by an indigenous Fijian, Timoci Uluivuda Bavadra, won the elections. This unexpected turn of events resurrected the old fears of an "Indian threat", reinforced by the fact that the majority of the coalition's members of parliament were Indo-Fijian, even though Bavadra had been named prime minister. The new government was in office barely a month when it was overthrown in May 1987 by a military coup supported by most indigenous Fijians, touching off an unprecedented wave of racial violence. In Suva, groups of indigenous Fijians attacked Indo-Fijian stores and property, beating their owners, and dozens of coalition supporters were arrested for demonstrating against the coup. Amelia Rokotuivuna, a member of the coalition and leader of the Young Women's Christian Association, was one of those arrested. She recalls that "during the interrogation following my arrest, I was very afraid of the officer in charge, not because he might hit me, but because I was aware that I inspired a great hate in him for having supported the Indians."

The prime minister and members of parliament for the coalition were detained, and the leader of the coup, Lieutenant

Colonel Sitiveli Rabuka, assumed power, claiming that he was thus preventing the "threats against law and order". The nationalist government did nothing but strengthen racial antagonism. For three years it ruled by decree, then in 1990 enacted a constitution forever establishing the political supremacy of indigenous Fijians over other communities living in the country. The resentment and anxiety this caused among the Indo-Fijian people is summed up in the words of a presentation by one of them to the Constitutional Review Commission in 1995: "Our people did not come here as colonizers but as workers, and it has been humiliating to be told four or five generations later that we have less rights than other communities in our own land."

International reaction to the 1987 coup and 1990 constitution was extremely adverse. Fiji was suspended from the Commonwealth until 1997. The military coup also brought negative economic consequences. Internal and external pressures grew for a prompt return to democracy, and in 1993 parliament voted to revise the constitution again.

But how is a multi-racial, multi-religious democracy to be built out of ethnic, religious and cultural diversity? How can the indigenous Fijians' fears of losing their lands and cultural identity to the "Indian threat" be allayed? How can Indo-Fijians regain their confidence that Fiji is their home and that they and their children will be able to live out their aspirations for a future with dignity? Many Fijians recognize that political approaches to these questions must be accompanied by intensive efforts within society as a whole.

Asaeli Lave is an indigenous Fijian, Mala Jagmohan is an Indo-Fijian. Both are journalists for the *Fiji Times*, one of Suva's two daily newspapers. Although they have a good collegial working relationship, they acknowledge that they have never visited each other's homes and that their families have never had any contact. "We are aware that we mix very little and that there is practically no social life between the different racial groups. We still need to overcome many stereotypes and prejudices. We always live aware of the social differences. Even to be admitted to a hospital we must indicate on the form what race we belong to. Although born in the same country, we have different names: indigenous Fijian ones and Indo-Fijian ones. These labels are difficult to defeat."

While the two journalists believe that the media can play an important role in education for a multi-racial democracy, they agree that the change of mentality regarding race must first be achieved in the families and schools. "Children are indoctrinated with stereotypes in their own families, due to either ignorance or fear or a mistaken nationalism. Schools should be mixed, but for students really to be willing to mix, first there should no longer be two teachers' unions, one for indigenous Fijians and the other for Indo-Fijians. How can we expect kids to accept studying together if we adults do not begin by setting the example?"

Both agree that a basic prerequisite to integration consists in everyone knowing his or her rights and obligations. They also feel that people must be encouraged to form citizen organizations in which all races are represented. "We must begin with small steps, but always walking together. It is a matter of giving way to a continuous process of democratization that earns the trust of all the people."

Radio journalist Francis Herman served as news director for the Island Network Corporation (INC) during the period before the new constitution was adopted in 1997. INC owns five radio stations that broadcast in three languages to all of the archipelago. Describing the role of radio in making the text of the new constitution known, Francis Herman says: "It is our duty to inform people about the different issues being discussed. But we tried to do so in the most objective and neutral way possible. We never gave opinions or commented on the issue. Our goal was for people to form their own opinions."

In the rural areas of Fiji, where 40 percent of the population lives, there are practically no telephones. INC regularly sends teams of journalists into the countryside and to the faraway islands to see the reality and talk to the people. Often they find that local leaders are taking advantage of the villagers' total lack of information to manipulate them.

One of the most serious cultural barriers to democracy in Fiji, according to Francis Herman, "is that we are above all very family-oriented. Therefore, we journalists tend to be very cautious when we report, because the worst thing that could happen to a person is to be rejected by his or her family. Another problem is that in our culture it is taboo to question a chief or religious leader. It is very difficult for people to understand that they *can* question a leader without implying disrespect to the authority being questioned. Since expressing disagreement is so difficult, people are often not honest and hide their true opinion."

Many experienced journalists left Fiji after the military coup in 1987. The journalists who succeeded them need to learn more about human rights, Francis Herman says. They need greater exposure to the world, and they need to gain more professional confidence. "In the Pacific, journalism as a career is not given much value, and this makes the work very difficult."

The Association of Young Lawyers of Fiji was one of the groups presenting proposals to the Citizens' Constitutional Forum (CCF) on different aspects of the new constitution. The association is a voluntary organization made up of about 30 lawyers from all races who have a progressive vision of Fiji's future and are struggling for a better society. Its educational campaign offers free legal counselling for people and organizations, as well as training on citizens' rights.

Two important elements, according to attorneys Marie A. Chan and Prem L. Narayan, are making known the new constitutional text, which protects freedom of the press, and creating a human rights commission to take account of international agreements. "Right now we are making the Universal Human Rights Declaration known, which is not widely familiar in our country. Democracy will work only if the population is educated for it. If people do not receive this civic education, they could easily be convinced by whoever is in power." These two young women attorneys fear that Fijian politicians are moving ahead too quickly with the new constitutional proposals without having done enough work at the grassroots level. They believe that the next ten years will be critical, as the changes proposed by the new constitution are tested again and again. "It will probably take one generation to change the way of thinking of Fijians, if the change finally does take place. What has happened is that certain culturally-based conducts have been accepted for too long; and these could have a significant negative weight at the time of implementing the changes. For example, it may be that human rights protection will work in individual cases, but it will be difficult to implement these provisions when customs and mores in the villages are involved. We will have to be willing to go beyond traditions and racial identity for them to have effect."

Efforts for a new constitutional text

The demand for a new constitutional text in Fiji was based on a conviction that in a multi-ethnic society all people contribute in one way or another to development and modernization, as well as the recognition that leaving either of the major ethnic groups out of decision-making would bring negative political, economic and social consequences. Thus in 1993 parliament voted unanimously to create a Constitutional Review Commission (CRC), whose functions were to establish the bases for a constitutional text, keeping in mind harmony between the races, national unity, human rights and the social and economic development of all citizens in the country.

The CRC was to have three members: an independent and neutral chair, one member representing the ruling party and one representing the main opposition party. Sir Paul Reeves was designated as chair, the first Maori governor general of Aotearoa New Zealand and a former Anglican archbishop; he was joined by a member of parliament for the ruling party, Tomasi Vakatora, and an Indo-Fijian historian living in Australia, Dr Brij Lal. Upon taking office in July 1995, the commission began a four-month period of consultation with the entire population, travelling to cities and rural areas throughout the country, by air, land and sea, holding public hearings in municipal buildings, schools or seated on mats in traditional community centres. In all, they received 470 oral and written submissions from individuals, churches, non-governmental organizations, ethnic groups, community organizations, trade unions and political parties.

"I am impressed by the seriousness and respect we are treated with everywhere, especially by people opposed to our work or by those who have a cynical vision of the results of our work," wrote Brij Val in an account of his work in the CRC. "I am excited about finding people in rural villages who have traveled from far and incurred expenses to come and make their submission to us. They come, they say what they think or want to contribute, and they go. Each one of them, regardless of their rank and origin, is given equal time and attention." The media avidly followed the process, with a summary of the commission's work presented day by day on television. At the end of the period of receiving the submissions, the members of the commission devoted six months to closed meetings to discuss and write up their recommendations.

The CRC recommendations defined a new constitutional model for Fiji in which all racial groups would feel safe in the land of their birth. All races should be able to participate in the country's government, and special protection should be granted for the rights of Fijians. The CRC recommendations were widely discussed, with voices raised in favour of and against them. Parliament designated a multi-party Joint Parliament Select Committee (JPSC) to analyze the report during the first four months of 1997. Despite some attempts to reject the work of the CRC altogether, the JPSC reached agreements on most of the CRC recommendations and on a formula for parliamentary representation that was accepted by all. This provides for 46 communal seats for the ethnic groups and 25 open seats. With support from the main parliamentary leaders and the Great Council of Chiefs, which gathers all the Fijian tribal chiefs, the new constitution was signed in July 1997, to go into effect in July 1998, looking ahead to general elections at the beginning of 1999.

Accompanying the work of politicians in formulating this new constitutional text was a broad movement of civil society. One of its expressions was the Citizens Constitutional Forum (CCF), formed by people from different political, social and religious backgrounds in 1994 after two national consultations on the topic of constitutional review. The goal of CCF was to promote a broad debate on issues of national interest from an inclusive and secular perspective. Committed to democracy and the defence of human rights, the members of CCF chose to remain independent from the political parties and from any ethnic identification. Support for the CCF came from the International Conciliation, a non-governmental organization headquartered in London which works on issues of conciliation in constitutional processes.

The CCF consulted with leaders and scholars throughout the country on such issues as indigenous rights, the electoral system, government accountability and transparency, power-sharing, negotiating and avoiding confrontation. It organized seminars and encounters and helped many groups in presenting their submissions to the CRC, besides making its own presentation. When the CRC report was published, CCF organized a national seminar to study and discuss it. Later it was invited to serve as a consultant for the JPSC.

"Our priority was to overcome ethnic divisions. We wanted to see the nation as a whole," points out Amelia Rokotuivuna of the Fiji YWCA. "It was important for the leaders to become acquainted with different ideas and to be able to consider that sharing power is a viable possibility in Fiji." With this in view the CCF did not hesitate to take on controversial issues, including the concern of indigenous Fijians that their group has an educational level inferior to the rest of the population, and the concern of Indo-Fijians about difficulty they have in gaining access to civil service positions.

"In Fiji it is very important to work with the leaders," explains CCF chair Vijay Naidu. "It is difficult for ordinary people to state easily what they think. There is this whole custom about respect towards the leaders, which creates a kind of 'culture of silence.' This is stronger among indigenous Fijians than among Indo-Fijians, who, since as they arrived in the country to work in the plantations and had to fend for themselves, tend to make decisions based on more independent criteria."

Vijay Naidu observes that "the consequences of colonial dominion do not disappear from one day to the next. Since some individuals and groups benefited during that period, they would like to perpetuate the structures that divided our society during the colonial period. It is not easy to make a conscious effort towards a multi-racial and multi-cultural society in Fiji. We have to make deliberate efforts to dismantle the segregationist scaffolding mounted so long ago. We know that many are going to resist its disappearance, and that the effort will thus take us some time."

The CCF supports three major initiatives for the future of the country. The first is promoting multi-culturalism through educational work to develop an appreciation of cultural diversity in which differences can be accepted without fear of destroying unity. The second is support for the creation of the Human Rights Commission contemplated under the new constitution and efforts to make people aware of the Bill of Rights. The third is making the population aware of the new office of ombudsman, a structure for monitoring and investigating government actions independently of the political power, and of how this office can defend citizen rights and ensure transparency from civil servants and the government.

"We have an excellent Bill of Rights in our new constitution," Vijay Naidu says. "But we must build a culture of respect for human rights and work particularly with the police, with lawyers, with the business community and with educators. Unfortunately, many still think of human rights as an issue that belongs to the Western world which has little to do with the interests of the different groups and communities in Fiji. Human rights have been violated in Fiji in favour of the prerogatives of a given ethnic group. That is why we must build bridges to develop a culture that appreciates the diversity that exists in our country. It is important that we learn to communicate through our different cultures, respecting their ethnicity with an integral vision."

To support its work of educating for democracy and human rights, CCF has published a series of widely used documents in English, Fijian and Hindi. Its annotated and illustrated brochure "Your Constitution, Your Rights" received support from the government and the prime minister attended its launch. The

Methodist Church has helped with translation of the texts into Fijian. Supported by churches and other organizations, the CCF subsequently undertook an educational campaign about the new voting system, including pamphlets on the electoral system and the meaning of power-sharing.

The new constitution introduces some important and complex changes into the Fijian electoral system. Voting will be mandatory, and citizens will have two votes: one to elect those who will occupy the communal seats for their ethnic community, the other to elect those who will occupy the open seats. In addition, they will also have to number candidates on a list in order of preference. According to the power-sharing provisions of the new constitution, the prime minister must select cabinet members from among all the political parties that obtain over 10 percent of the seats in the House of Representatives. To involve all members of parliament in political decisions and governance, five standing committees in the House of Representatives will be in charge of formulating policies and monitoring all areas of government. In this way the political confrontation that has poisoned ethnic relations in Fiji will be replaced by a system of governance based on cooperation.

Land remains a critical issue. About 96 percent of the land in Fiji is communally owned; and the Native Land Trust Board watches over the interests of traditional owners. Many Indo-Fijian farmers who rent their fields for sugar cane production will have to renew their leases in the year 2000. The stability of the sugar cane industry, which is critical for the country's economy, depends in large measure on an amicable resolution of the lease renewals; and polarization around this issue could obviously create serious new ethnic tensions. Fortunately, political leaders agree that a mechanism similar to that adopted during the revision of the constitution could be developed in order to allow a broad debate and the participation of all social sectors in this discussion. For its part, CCF is preparing technical studies and educational programmes in order to respond to the land issue before tensions build up.

In granting special protection to the rights of the indigenous Fijians, including the Rotumans, the new constitution stipulates that all the various laws protecting the traditional rights of the indigenous Fijians can be changed only through a majority vote of the members of both houses of parliament, including the majority of the 14 senators who represent the traditional government body of the indigenous Fijians, the Great Council of Chiefs (the *Bose Levu Vakaturaga*). This Council designates the president and vice-president and can also remove them from office.

Cultural dialogue among Fijians

The welcoming ceremony begins with two Indo-Fijian women approaching the newcomers and placing a beautiful garland of marigolds – a flower with special significance in the Hindu tradition – around their necks. With candles and incense in their hands, they begin a gentle dance around the visitors, offering them both light and warmth. When this dance has ended, the young indigenous Fijians who have been watching silently, seated on the ground, begin to beat the drums. One of them prepares the *yaqona* (*kava*), a traditional drink made of vegetable roots, and serves it to the visitors in a coconut container, which is passed around. This is followed by the rhythmic clapping of hands, a sign of approval in Fijian culture.

The solemn combination of elements from both indigenous and Indo-Fijian traditions in this ceremony shows something of the nature of the cultures that co-exist in Fiji. It is part of a dialogue between the two cultures which began in 1990 when the Columban Fathers organized the first two-week inter-cultural course to encourage better relations between the different communities in Fiji. Out of this course grew People for International Awareness (PIA), an organization that promotes dialogue, tolerance and mutual understanding across cultures. PIA organizes inter-cultural workshops and promotes relations between the ethnic groups in educational institutions and multi-ethnic organizations. A key element of its work is training public officials and teachers by giving them first-hand experience of participating in an inter-cultural group, hoping they will see how critical understanding between the different cultures is and will then incorporate what they have learned into their daily work.

"The workshops help people to speak openly about their prejudices and feelings and to listen to what others have to say about that," according to Douglas Akehurst, a Roman Catholic priest who teaches at the St Vincent de Paul seminary on the outskirts of Suva and has been very involved in developing PIA. "At the beginning of PIA's work, workshops were held with leaders, politicians and social activists. Now we have begun to work with teachers, because we believe it is essential for our children to grow up with open, receptive and respectful minds towards the cultures that exist on the island."

Sister Shakuntla, an Indo-Fijian, points out how important it is in mixed parishes to work on pastoral counselling and home visits. "Little by little, people start to become used to the idea of receiving persons from other races in their homes, to talk to them about their problems and to trust their spiritual counsel," she says. Jioji Bilowalu, an indigenous Fijian seminary student, recalls the initial difficulties he faced when assigned to work in an Indo-Fijian community. "I could not understand the way people were and their family customs. But it was important to share the most daily and simple aspects of the community's life. In a few days, I felt more comfortable and was able to begin to appreciate different aspects from their culture and their way of putting the gospel teachings into practice."

With support from the Roman Catholic archdiocese of Suva, Fr Frank Hoare of PIA has prepared a workbook with inter-cultural exercises for the classroom, to be used in Catholic schools. Based on a creative learning process that awakens the students' interest, these exercises are a good tool for breaking down prejudices and beginning to create trustful relationships between the different ethnic groups. Through the workbook, which is also used in non-Catholic schools, students experience cultural shock situations that help them to reflect on how they relate with other ethnic groups in daily life. They are thus able to see the danger of being guided by stereotypes and prejudices and they learn about the advantages of cooperation rather than of competition.

The dialogue between religions

When the military coup rocked Fiji in 1987, leaders of the different religious groups issued a call to all people of faith to pray for the good of the country and to join efforts to find a path to understanding. Four months later, a group of Hindus, Muslims and Christians began to meet informally to pray and respond to the dilemmas created by the heightened ethnic tensions. Hosted by the different religious organizations, these discussions allowed participants to explore together how the spiritual resources of each of their traditions might contribute to healing rather than aggravating ethnic relations. These meetings gave birth to Interfaith Search Fiji, based on the model of the Multifaith Centre of Birmingham, England. The ten religious organizations which founded it set as their goal to "find ways of building bridges of respect and understanding between people of different religious traditions".

In a context in which most of the indigenous Fijian population is Christian and most of the Indo-Fijian population Hindu, Interfaith Search has sought to create a climate in which suspicion could be set aside and trust and respect between people of different religious traditions emphasized. Members of the group have come to learn more about their own religion through interaction with people of other confessions. Together, they have learned how to work effectively against misconceptions and prejudices. Interfaith Search also presented a submission to the CRC underscoring the importance of ensuring that the multi-religious nature of Fijian society would be respected under the new constitution. The new Bill of Rights guarantees that religious freedom is protected as one of the basic rights of Fijian citizens.

To enrich the dialogue between the religions Interfaith Search decided to focus on one subject each year in its public meetings. On special occasions it has organized inter-faith prayer meetings, such as the celebrations of 150 years of Roman Catholic missionary work in the country and of 25 years of Fijian independence. It also held a public ceremony affirming creation and protesting against the nuclear tests in the Pacific.

"Our work is careful. We bear in mind that religious freedom is a very sensitive issue and that the possibility of a dialogue between the different faiths depends on a climate of mutual respect," points out Tessa MacKenzie, coordinator of Interfaith Search. The interfaith religious services have been held so far in Christian churches or outdoors. While there was considerable criticism of these celebrations at first, people have gradually begun to accept them. "Every religious community is invited to participate in the service with a two- or three-minute contribution. We do not want anyone to feel obligated to pray according to a different religious confession, but we do ask people to come willing to listen in prayer to what other confessions express. In this way we encourage respect and a better understanding of other people's religiosity."

Over the years, Interfaith Search Fiji has created an interesting movement within the different religious confessions, opening them up to dialogue and tolerance. It has undertaken educational work to create awareness in adults and young people of the need to respect religious freedom and accept religious diversity. While the arson attacks against Hindu temples which have taken place in Fiji in the past are attributed to political rather than religious confrontation, everyone recognizes that this is a sensitive matter and that careful work is needed to ensure that no one's religion is attacked under any circumstance.

The Fiji Council of Churches has made its own contribution to promoting religious freedom in the country, emphasizing in its submission to the CRC the need to form a pluralist nation and to strengthen an inclusive society. From the side of the Roman Catholic Church, which makes up about 15 percent of the population (half the priests are Fijian, the rest foreign), Archbishop Mataca of Suva was very active in supporting the social movement opposed to the 1987 coup. He encouraged Catholics to carry out interfaith encounters in each parish to allow indigenous Fijians and Indo-Fijians to share their experiences during the coup, learn of each other's suffering and frustrations and nurture hope for a better future. This programme helped to create a climate of mutual understanding in the crisis situation. The Roman Catholic Church also made a submission to the CRC after extensive consultation with the entire Catholic community. A task force worked on the final document, which developed a vision of Fiji as a multi-cultural and multi-religious country in which all citizens have the same rights and obligations, without discrimination of any kind.

The Methodist Church is the largest in Fiji, with over 300,000 members. Its influence is specially strong in the villages. Since the two military coups of 1987, it has been a major actor in the political events and relationships. On the day of the first coup, Rev. Josateki Koroi, president of the Methodist Church, contacted fellow church leaders and issued an statement condemning the coup, which was broadcast on the same day and published in the newspapers the next day. However, tensions within the Methodist Church grew during 1987 and 1988. The general secretary, Rev. Manasa Lasaro, was an outspoken supporter of the coups and Fiji nationalism in the name of the Fijian people and their chiefs, while Rev. Koroi was speaking out strongly and consistently against the coups. In 1988, the Methodist Conference elected new leadership, which engaged actively in support of the political party that led the coups and carried forward Fijian nationalistic aspirations. The Methodist submission to the CRC was a clear illustration of this. Nevertheless, individual Methodist laypersons and ministers continued to dissent from the position of the church leadership. In 1995, a new president was elected, Dr Ilaitia Sevati Tuwere, and he is leading the Methodist Church in a new direction.

The contribution of women

Arlene Griffen believes that the feminist movement in the Pacific has generally been more concerned with issues of community and national development than with political power struggles. Nevertheless, she points out that feminists have questioned the patriarchal system in their community work and have worked in favour of the poor and marginal. "Women have played an important role in bringing about the political changes taking place in Fiji at this moment," according to Professor Griffen, who teaches literature at the South Pacific University in

Suva. After the military coup, many took part in the civil movements calling for a prompt return to a pluralist democracy.

There are cultural barriers in Fiji that hinder women's active participation in the public sphere. Although some tribal chiefs are women, they have attained this position only because they belong to a family with high social standing. It is not common for a woman to speak in public meetings, either in the indigenous Fijian or in the Indo-Fijian cultures. However, women leaders have arisen in recent years from the middle and lower levels of society. The multi-ethnic, multi-party organization Women in Politics has been involved in significant work at the community and local council levels. Taking advantage of the active participation of women in the development of their villages and communities, it has encouraged the selection of women as delegates to provincial and municipal councils.

"Women are respected because they are always in touch with the grassroots and defend their claims," observes Lily King, project officer for Women in Politics. "At this moment there is a good participation of women at the middle level of leadership and in the district councils." Three women have been elected as members of parliament. "It is a small percentage, when you take into account that there are 70 seats," Lily King says. "In Fiji, 48 percent of the population is made up of women, and we feel we should have more representatives of our gender in the house. We hope to have 10 women gain seats in the next election."

In its programme of democratic education aimed at women, Women in Politics organizes three types of workshops under the name "Let's Change Fiji". One is intended for a maximum of 100 women and deals with issues related to political participation; a second involves training groups of 50 women in electoral matters related to the new constitutional provisions; the third, for groups of 10 women, trains trainers to create awareness of the political changes needed in Fiji. Some women would like to form their own political party, but insist that it should not be gender-biased. Others feel that women should participate in a party that defends the enforcement of human rights above all.

Lily King believes that an important contribution women can make to the peace process is denouncing domestic violence, which is culturally accepted in Fiji and "has an impact of the lives of women at all levels. A battered woman or one who is psychologically pressured by her spouse will never be able to vote independently or participate actively in favor of social change." Another contribution has to do with monitoring the management of resources. "Most of the poor are women. And we are convinced that a good distribution of resources would put an end to many social differences that create frustration and generate tension and racial violence." Arlene King's organization has thus worked to strengthen women financially, helping them to create small businesses in which they can augment family income while taking care of their families.

The Fiji Women's Rights Movement, founded in 1986, has been working in favour of laws advancing the rights of women, particularly in the area of violence against them. Its coordinator, Gina Houng Lee, believes that legal norms in Fiji do not adequately consider the economic and labour rights of women, nor do they sufficiently censure sexual assaults committed against them. This movement has been active in providing training on issues related to the rights of women included in the Convention Against All Forms of Discrimination Against Women and in putting pressure on parliament to enact legislation for women's human rights. Gina Houng Lee believes that just laws regarding these matters would contribute to social peace by creating more harmonious relations at work and in the home, less economic marginalization and a more equal social situation for women.

The Fiji Women's Crisis Centre has also been working since 1984 on strengthening women's rights and publicly advocating the idea that no one should inflict violence on women or children under any circumstance whatever. The centre is part of a network of similar centres in 13 other islands of the Pacific. It provides counseling and support services, community education, training, information and research. Its newsletter on violence against women in the Pacific region circulates extensively. One of its main programmes is devoted to women who have been the victims of violence and to exerting pressure on the authorities to create shelters for battered women. The centre also made submissions to the CFC on matters related to women's rights to land and to equal civil and social rights.

Different sectors of the population in Fiji have worked arduously to achieve peace between the different ethnic groups, bearing in mind above all a constitutional framework which will allow the consolidation of a multi-cultural and multi-ethnic society. This process has involved several years of debate at all levels of society and from different perspectives: political, social, religious, cultural and gender. Many believe that it will take a long time to put the new provisions into effect. Yet there is also optimism, based on the conviction that such a period of transition will be worthwhile if the foundations can be laid for a solid nation, in which people do not feel the need to resort to violence to assert their rights.

8. Kingston

"Why shoot my gun?", the young man thought as he ran to the seashore. There he felt calmer. Sitting down on the sand, he began to throw stones into the water. As he watched the ripples that formed each time one of the stones hit the surface of the water, a thousand thoughts crossed his mind: the theft of the television set, the chase, the wounded thief, the showdown between those members of his crew who wanted revenge and those who did not, the revenge, his attempts to mediate, the unbearable wave of continuing of violence. Two months earlier he had attended a workshop of leaders and neighbours in the Bennetland district. They had worked together on different ways of dealing with neighbourhood violence and overcoming the cyclical feuding which caused daily confrontations and bloodshed. Now things had gone too far. The showdowns between old friends had become intolerable.

He spent a long time by the sea. When he returned, he went directly to the S-Corner Clinic to get help. He had not wanted to get involved in the fray, and now he was no longer part of either of the two opposing groups. What was worse, his girlfriend had left him because he was no longer willing to commit petty crimes to support himself financially. He would rather die of hunger than steal, he told the staff at the clinic. But finding work for a young man from one of the marginal neighbourhoods of Kingston is not easy. Even if he has all the necessary qualifications, employers are not interested once they find out where he comes from.

But this young man was willing to change his life around, and he knew that the staff at the clinic would do all they could to help him. During the workshop, he had learned many things. He had also come to envision something new – a neighbourhood without violence. A few days later, he received the good news that a non-governmental organization was willing to hire him as a watchman. He would be able to earn a livelihood with a stable job. His hopes for a life without violence had begun to take on shape.

Violence marks daily life in places like Bennetland, an extremely poor inner-city district in Kingston with a population of about 6000. Most of it stems from the people's low income and lack of resources. Unemployment affects 40 percent of the residents, and the figure is higher among youth. Those who do have jobs generally work for minimum wages, amounting to 800 Jamaican dollars (US$22) a week, barely enough to cover basic household expenses, since 75 percent of it must go to buying food, usually of poor quality, which means their diet is poor in proteins and vitamins.

Jamaica has 2.5 million inhabitants. During much of its colonial past, a good part of its people lived in slavery. For almost 20 years after its independence from Great Britain in 1962 the country enjoyed a certain economic and political stability, which was reflected in the behaviour of the population. The police patrolled the streets with nothing more than a baton at the waist, since all that was involved was restraining "a few rude boys" armed with knives.

But political violence at the end of the 1970s and the beginning of the 1980s brought about economic instability, which in turn resulted in an upsurge of violence. In 1980 this violence claimed 600 victims for political reasons, and 289 for other motives. The number of homicides was similar in 1996, except that political violence is now virtually non-existent. Moreover, 65 percent of the crimes are committed in Kingston, making it one of the most violent cities in the Americas. Experts say the level of violent deaths there has surpassed the threshold of tolerance and that the frustrated and fearful people can only respond with more violence when faced with any situation that represents a danger to their frail domestic, neighbourhood or social stability.

The S-Corner Clinic

A group of neighbours ran to the nearby church to look for Pastor Ledgister. They were afraid that another bloody showdown was about to erupt in the neighbourhood and they wanted someone to help them resolve the conflict. The minister hurried to go with them. As they approached the boundary that divides the neighbourhood into territories according to groups of influence, the people on the other side thought they were coming to attack them and prepared to defend themselves. In this moment of high tension, Pastor Ledgister was helped by staff of the S-Corner Clinic to clarify the situation. While the director of the clinic and others encouraged the group of neighbours to talk, Pastor Ledgister prayed. After this encounter in April 1997, there were 20 further meetings between leaders and neighbours determined to ensure peace. Since then, there has been an implicit cease-fire in the area. Residents can walk along the lanes and streets of the neighbourhood without fear of attack.

The S-Corner Clinic was founded in August 1990 in Bennetland, Kingston, by a Jamaican medical doctor and a US Peace Corps volunteer. The medical service began to operate in the St Peter Claver Church and was later moved to a nearby building abandoned in 1980 when its owners left the country, fearing an imminent socialist government. The clinic's services were later expanded to include an educational programme for children and teenagers and another one for community development. The latest programme to be started is one for mediation and the peaceful resolution of conflicts. Funding for the S-Corner Clinic comes from both Jamaica and abroad, including the World Council of Churches and the United Nations Development Programme.

Angela Stultze-Crawlle, a Rastafarian social worker, is the clinic's current director. Her own community spirit and commitment are reflected in the dedication of her staff. Resources are administered by the book. Those who work here must be imbued with special courage, since this is one of the most difficult and dangerous neighbourhoods in Kingston.

Bennetland is known popularly as a garrison community – a neighbourhood built to serve the political interests of the People's National Party (PNP) and the Jamaica Labour Party (JLP) by attracting the votes and support of the poor urban population during the 1980s. There are twelve such districts in Kingston, and all have serious problems of violence. At that time, the dons or zone chiefs acted as delegates for the politicians, imposing their own rules and rough justice. Their actions, though severe in terms of discipline and when aimed at political adversaries, provided a measure of protection for the community, since one of the most important rules was never to attack the community itself. Delinquent acts were harshly punished.

Major trafficking in small arms began in the inner-city during the 1980s. At first these weapons belonged to the adults in power. In recent years the places of power in the garrison communities have been taken over by corner crew youth, who mark out their territories and defend those boundaries aggressively. The result is a situation of constant violence which the local population recognizes as war. Those who fight in these territorial battles are called "warriors" or "soldiers", and their main concern is to ensure that no stranger enters into their area of influence. The gang violence walls in the neighbours, terrorized and victimized by their own youth.

Its services and its work for peace have earned the S-Corner Clinic respect in the neighbourhood, and it has been able to provide a neutral space where people from other districts can also be attended to. Only once has the clinic been robbed; and the reaction in the neighbourhood was so angry that the stolen items were returned a few hours later.

In Bennetland, 55 percent of the residents are women, and most of them are heads of households. The majority of people work on their own as artisans or in different sectors of the construction business. Many of the women are domestic workers or cook food to sell on the streets of the surrounding neighbourhood.

The clinic provides outpatient facilities for the population, preventive care through vaccinations and health education, and mother-child care, which is especially important because young people form couples at a very early age and the average number of children per family is 4.5. It is not unusual to meet a 12- or 13-year-old girl with her child in arms; and there are said to be as many as a thousand 26-year-old grandmothers in Jamaica – which implies an important shift of roles within the family. While many of the couples are not married legally, common-law unions are respected and lasting.

The educational work of the S-Corner Clinic includes HAPPY (Homework Assistance Participatory Programme for Youths) and the Grassroots College. HAPPY offers children and adolescents between 9 and 15 daily help with schoolwork. It is staffed by volunteers – one teacher for every ten students. Besides helping children with their homework, the programme seeks to build up their self-esteem and self-confidence so that they will become actively involved in the learning process at school.

The Grassroots College is for young persons between 16 and 25 who have not finished high school. After completing this one-year programme, students can enter Human Employment and Resource Training (HEART), a government service which refers them to other institutions for training in nursing, masonry, carpentry, sewing, hairdressing and other skills. About 90 percent of those who finish at the Grassroots College find jobs.

Diane Peart, who attended the Grassroots College and then took a course in practical nursing, is now part of the four-person team of community health workers at the S-Corner Clinic. In addition to consultations at the clinic, these health workers go into the neighbourhood regularly to visit homes and monitor the health of the population. They ensure that all children receive their immunizations on time, that they are being fed correctly and that family hygiene standards are adequate to prevent the most common diseases in the area. They also monitor the health of senior citizens and request medical care for them as necessary.

Once a month the S-Corner Community Council meets. The Council has 50 members, most of them community leaders, committed to improving living conditions in the neighbourhood, which is crisscrossed with narrow lanes dividing one block from another and has few common areas. Most houses are surrounded by two-metre high metal sheeting, which protects and isolates them but also gives a gloomy and depressing appearance to the neighbourhood. The Council approached this situation by organizing a competition in which residents were invited to paint the metal sheeting in an attractive way.

Recognizing that many of the neighbourhood's health problems were due to the lack of sanitary services and drinking water, the Council developed a plan in which residents themselves approached the local municipality to petition for the laying of pipes for potable water and the construction of latrines for groups of families. Twenty-three members of the community took part in the work. Almost 80 percent of the people now have sanitary services in the form of VIP latrines (Ventilated, Improved and Permanent). A quarter of the houses now have potable running water and the rest has access to public taps.

Sport also plays a role in integrating the community. The S-Corner Clinic encourages the formation of teams to participate in tournaments organized by Fathers Incorporated. Soccer is the favourite sport, especially since the Jamaican national team qualified for the World Cup in France in 1998. The "Reggae Boys" are a good example for many young people, since most of the team members came from poor neighbourhoods in conflict and demonstrated that with effort and discipline it is possible to reach the international level in a sport much loved in Jamaica. The tournaments in which the S-Corner teams take part allow dozens of youth from different districts to develop a spirit of camaraderie, far from the fights of the corner crews, and to get to know each other without prejudices or false barriers.

The Bennetland neighbourhood also decided to form a Peace Committee, with recognized members of the community, including a minister of the Church of God, a Catholic priest, the director of the clinic, the school principal and an advisor. More than once this committee has organized meetings at which sectors in conflict can meet and set aside their violent attitudes. The members of the committee are very realistic, avoiding long-term promises that would be difficult to fulfill in favour of short-term, feasible goals – like working to maintain peace in the neighbourhood for one month. There are ups and downs in this work, but the committee has continued to demonstrate enormous tenacity and dedication.

"It is a long process," says Peace Committee member Horace Levy. "People can change their conduct, but I think it will be difficult to achieve lasting peace as long as the lack of employment and the bad living conditions of the people are not resolved. We do not deny that there is a high crime rate in the neighbourhood, but we can say that most of the people are not violent by nature, but that the social deterioration often pushes them to act violently in the face of living conditions that have become unbearable."

Community development enables peace

Elsewhere in Kingston, educational and preventive health care tasks are being carried out by the St Patrick's Foundation, a Catholic organization, and the Anglican Church's St Andrew Settlement Programme. Both carry out community development programmes that encourage neighbourhood peace initiatives.

Fabian Brown of the St Patrick's Foundation says that it is society's failure to respond to people's basic needs that generates violent situations in the neighbourhoods. The Foundation's centres in five inner-city Kingston neighbourhoods – Waterhouse, Olympic Gardens, Riverton City, Calaloo Mews and Seaview Gardens – offers programmes in adult literacy, job training, care of senior citizens, health care and workshops in different trades. Besides these, it operates community work programmes to encourage participation and solutions to different problems. Before planning and beginning any programmes, the Foundation meets with neighbourhood representatives and studies how to respond to its specific needs.

"Very often a neighbourhood with a bad reputation is stigmatized, and it is hard for people there to surmount the situation this creates," says Fabian Brown. "At the Foundation's centres we work so that people, in addition to improving their educational level and preparing to find a job, can also recover their dignity and confidence in themselves. We encourage teamwork and community work so that people can begin to trust each other and begin to see that they can improve their neighbourhood. We also support peace talks between opposing groups and work particularly with children and adolescents at high risk."

The St Andrew Settlement has been working since 1965 in Majesty Gardens, a "garrison community" of 7000 inhabitants, which has been afflicted by violence and hopelessness. The project has a day-care school with 120 students, a senior citizens' club, a library, a youth club sponsored by the Jamaica Constabulary Force and a free medical and dental service attended by volunteer professionals. A multi-purpose room, divided into several classrooms during the week, becomes a sanctuary for worship and church education on Sundays.

A few steps away from the original apartment buildings in Majesty Gardens, a new housing project is being built through a self-help system and low-interest mortgage loans. So far 25 of a planned 40 new houses have gone up. The houses share a common area where the children can play, and all are well-kept and neatly decorated – in stark contrast to the unpainted, poorly maintained and half-destroyed buildings elsewhere in the neighbourhood.

"The main problem in this area is unemployment," says Pastor Vivette Jennings. "Most people work in the informal economy, as artisans or street vendors, but their income is very low and this causes much frustration. Young people often get into trouble and many people think they will be better off financially if they steal.

"This is a very closed community. The people all belong to the same political party, and it is rare for them to go to other parts of the city. Men usually do not go out much. There is turf violence and problems increase around the time of elections. When the younger generation becomes involved in violence they are often totally irrational; and it is very difficult to talk with them."

Vivette Jennings recognizes that the parents are interested in their children's education. They insist on their going to grade school, and most at least begin high school, though the dropout rate is very high. In spite of this, some young people from this neighbourhood have been able to study at the university. Geraldine Simmons, who works helping her mother wash clothes, is studying to be an English teacher. Vivette Jennings believes that it is especially important to help such young people who, without leaving the neighbourhood, prove that it is possible to chose a different path for one's life.

Criminality and youth

During the 1960s the crime rates in Jamaica were comparable to those of other Caribbean islands. Subsequently, the situation worsened, because of the political violence which placed a large number of weapons in the hands of people, and because of the accelerated deterioration of living conditions, aggravated by the "structural adjustment policies" imposed by international financial institutions. Professor Anthony Harriot, an internal security advisor for the government, mentions an additional factor: the role of Jamaica's colonial past, whose socio-economic structures of inequality, poverty and social segmentation, exacerbated by racism, remained intact after independence.

Towards the end of the 1970s, Jamaica became a cheap labour market which did nothing to train its workers. Dissatisfied with the very low wages, many people preferred to drop their jobs and work independently. Between 1977 and 1988, wages fell nearly 14 percent in real terms, while the government's allocation for social services such as health care and education was being reduced – from 22 percent of the total budget in 1977 to 17 percent in 1992. The resulting rapid drop in living standards led to an extraordinary growth of independent labour and the informal economy. The male work force fell from 84 percent in 1985 to 74.6 percent in 1993, with the greatest decline coming among men under 25. Surveys showed that 53 percent of the economically active population preferred not having a full-time job, since they were able to earn more in the informal economy. Many of these latter activities involved crime.

An additional important factor has been the growth of the drug trade. Anthony Harriot points out that during the 1980s, more and more Jamaicans, faced with the social and economic crisis of the island, began to be involved in the foreign trade of cannabis, the consumption of which is socially accepted in Jamaica. Soon complete organizations were formed to traffic in dangerous narcotics, and they now compete with the other large bands of international traffickers operating in Europe and North America. The nature of the drug trade led to a rapid increase in the number of small arms – from revolvers to automatic rifles – coming into the country, at very accessible prices.

This has changed the nature of crime in Jamaica. According to police statistics, crimes against property have fallen by 49 percent over the last 20 years, while violent crimes have increased by 30 percent. Since most crimes are committed by heavily armed individuals, the risk of death is very high. More than 20 percent of the homicides are related to skirmishes between gangs, and in 64 percent of the cases, the victims knew their assailants. Homicides are often followed by the mutilation of the victim, which is seen as a way of terrorizing the competition.

The political violence at the beginning of the 1980s had a significant impact on these developments, fostering violent confrontations and in a sense giving legitimacy to the resort to violence. "The inner-city population was used cynically by the politicians," Horace Levy points out. "The people were manipulated with false promises and then they felt cheated. The residents feel that the rest of the population does not respect them, and this increases their aggressiveness. Violence was interpreted as a viable path to resolve conflicts."

The shift of a large portion of the young work force into circles related to the drug trade worsened the situation. Competition over territorial dominion and the settling of accounts between gangs led to an increase of armed confrontations in the streets, with the inevitable toll of victims. The situation is so serious in some parts of inner-city Kingston that no one from outside ever goes into the neighbourhood after 6:00 p.m. Further complicating matters is the fact that many police stations also close their doors at 6:00 p.m. Thus the inner city has thus become a no man's land and its streets are under the rule of gangs and traffickers.

Urban youth are involved in a disproportionate number of these bloody confrontations. According to 1993 homicide statistics, 65 percent of the victims were under 25, 70 percent lived in a city and 89 percent were unemployed or independent males. The police have identified about 3,000 "hard" criminals. The rate of criminal recidivism has reached 60 percent, and third-time offenders now account for half of the prison population. "Most young people are afraid of leaving their neighbourhoods, because if they do so they will be discriminated against or because they could become the victims of an attack from an opposing band," says Horace Levy. "It upsets them that the place they come from is a reason for discrimination."

In the Jamaican culture, many young males feel pressure from the family to go out and look for work as soon as they turn 15. Fewer and fewer young men are completing high school studies, much less those who make it as far as the university. This perpetuates their status as unskilled labourers, unable to find any job other than a low-paying one, which means they are constantly tempted by the informal economy or the drug trade. Horace Levy also cites the negative influence on young people by the media: "Violent conduct is nourished by the messages of television series, in which everything is resolved with blows and revenge is encouraged and accepted as an honourable solution."

Violence can also be encouraged by the police force. In general, people are afraid of reporting crimes to the police, since those suspected of being police informers may be murdered or have their houses burned down. Many observers think it is the police themselves who alert the corner crews when charges are filed against one of their members, so that they will get revenge. This generates a great deal of confusion among the people, who do not know who to go to for justice.

The government is trying to make changes in the role and perception of the police. One recent initiative is the creation of a Mediation Unit in the police force. Fourteen police officers have received special training to deal with conflicts in the neighbourhoods and schools, domestic violence and disputes between landlords and tenants. A pilot programme of conflict resolution, in which police work with special teams of professional advisors, has had a 70 percent success rate. The Mediation Unit also offers an educational programme in schools, churches and citizen groups. "We think this type of police programme can help build a more positive relationship with the people and the police," says Constable Michael Gooden of the Mediation Unit. "The people also feel safer in seeing that the police is dealing with these problems and trying to resolve matters without confrontation. For the police themselves this is also a very positive experience, because a different kind of relationship develops with the people, one based on respect and trust."

Horace Levy disagrees with the idea that special police forces must be formed to control the corner crews. He thinks these groups would change their behaviour if they were treated properly and had an opportunity to get out of the cycle of violence in which they are trapped. Jamaicans are vivacious by nature and tend to show initiative. That is why it is so important to offer possibilities for change. Levy also believes that inner city youth are aware that their situation is to a large extent due to the lack of adequate education and the absence of parental guidance. Many grow up in families with only one parent, usually the mother. Many parents are often too young to take responsibility for their adolescent children. Moreover, the behaviour of many adults borders on the criminal.

Peta-Anne Baker, a social worker and university professor, agrees with Levy that most young Jamaicans have a great deal of initiative and would like to accomplish something in their lives. "Most of them admit they could achieve much more and that they want to be well prepared for that," she says. "That is why we should be alert to what happens in the schools. There is an enormous potential in our hands, but if we do not take advantage of the opportunity, many will quit studying, frustrated because their aspirations are not fulfilled." Peta-Anne Baker believes that it is very important to provide community leaders with direction. Unlike the politicians, who have often manipulated the needs of the neighbourhoods to further their own interests, teachers and social workers, who enjoy a certain amount of recognition in the neighbourhoods, can provide support and advice.

In some schools intervention by the community in favour of the students' interests has had a positive effect in encouraging the young people to continue their studies. One of the most serious problems with the educational system in Jamaica is that enrollment is high but attendance is low. "In view of the conditions of many schools in our cities, we could say that the teachers who do not migrate and the students who survive this system are true heroes," says Peta-Anne Baker. "Unfortunately, the teaching profession is no longer valued by the people and by teachers themselves. The low salaries and the state of the schools, with inferior and poorly equipped buildings, are part of the problem. We also need to improve education in terms of contents. We must also inspire confidence and dignity in the students. Most have a negative image about themselves. Even in their own families they are told they are not good for anything, that they will never achieve anything important. It is essential that they be able to express their most intimate aspirations, that they feel capable of reaching their goals and of demonstrating they have the will to do so. The cultural and spiritual content of education should point to us caring about other people and respecting their dignity as creative beings, capable of making a contribution to society."

Recognizing this creativity of young people and their desire to participate in the community, the Mustard Seed Project, a Catholic community development initiative, began an FM radio station for young people three years ago, "Roots FM 96.1: the Voice of the Inner City." Now independent, the station has an enthusiastic and youthful staff who have received special training in technical operations and programming. The staff themselves all live in the inner city. Programmes include general information and features on topics of special interest to youth, as well as religious programmes run by young people. The project was set up with the assistance of UNESCO, which donated the basic equipment. "The radio station now belongs to the people," says Roots FM director Tony Young. "That is how it acquires legitimacy in the community. In addition, it allows the voices of many young people to be validated, as they can express their opinion about the issues that most concern them. This also nourishes the self-esteem of our people."

Church work for peace in the inner city

"The people trust the churches and hold ministers and priests in high esteem," says Angela Stultze-Crawlle. "When there are problems in the neighbourhood, they don't hesitate to go to a representative of the church. When the gangs in Bennetland were on the verge of confrontation, they called the pastor, because they trusted that he would be a good mediator."

The credibility of the churches of different confessions and denominations grows out of the work they carry out. Many feel that the churches should have even more effective presence in the inner city, particularly in the pastoral field. "People need guidance, someone to walk with them," says Vivette Jennings. "Life in these neighbourhoods is harsh, and young people don't always have an adult figure they can trust. One has to be willing to listen a lot to people and also provide advice regarding daily life and spiritual struggles."

"Many people feel violence is unavoidable," points out Ashley Smith, a professor in the United Theological College of the West Indies in Kingston and chair of Interfaith Fellowship. "There are many Christians who have a fatalistic and apocalyptic interpretation of what is occurring and who feel that the violence present in society is only an indication that the coming of Christ is near. Others, particularly in the mainline Protestant churches, feel that violence is a problem of the poor and that people need to be taken out of the violent neighbourhoods, instead of changing the economic and social conceptions that lead to violent situations. The middle class, which forms the majority in these churches, wants to be physically safe, so they hide behind bars, watchdogs and security guards in their neighbourhoods."

Ashley Smith notes that many people in the marginalized neighbourhoods are interested in two religious contacts: one with a Pentecostal church to obtain salvation, the other with a mainline church to obtain a scholarship or a letter of recommendation for a prospective employer. Parents often have their children baptized in a mainline church because the denomination can give them a certain status; later, as adults, they are re-baptized in the Pentecostal church. A letter of recommendation from the minister of a church in which the majority of the members are middle- or upper-class means a great deal to a resident from a poor neighbourhood. Women heads of poor households will join a middle class-church hoping that if their children get into trouble they can find help from a lawyer or from the pastor.

But many things are changing on the church scene in Jamaica, says Ashley Smith. Pentecostal pastors who once rejected any type of intellectual formation now attend seminaries and are interested in obtaining their degree in theology. The number of women pastors has grown in all the denominations. "Women pastors are usually city women, and are therefore very active, willing to work with the congregations and familiar with how to exercise authority," says Ashley Smith. "But it is also extremely important to have good male figures among the pastors. We find many families in the inner cities where there is no father. Young people need male role models in which they can see themselves reflected – responsible men who work hard, who are faithful to their wives, who keep their promises."

Ashley Smith believes that Rastafarian men tend to set a good example for youth by their dedication to their families. The Rastafarians are probably best known around the world for their reggae music, particularly through Bob Marley and other famous artists, who have often been generous in their support for the poor and outspoken in their advocacy of peace. Both men and women from this group – to which 10 percent of the population belongs and whose symbols and customs the vast majority of Jamaicans accept – are opposed to sexual promiscuity. They preach equality and social justice and condemn the unfair distribution of wealth. The Rastafarians respect Jesus Christ, but they do not believe in life after death and hold that one must rather struggle for a better life in this world. Their conviction that the former emperor of Ethiopia, Haile Selassie, was a reincarnation of Christ and a direct descendant of King David means that they attach great importance to Jamaicans' African roots, which has had a significant impact in the search for Jamaican cultural origins and identity. Even the churches are beginning to include music and songs with an Afro-Caribbean rhythm in their services.

One problem of growing concern for the churches is domestic violence. Ashley Smith underscores the importance of preparing ministers to play an effective role in preventing domestic violence and in caring for those affected by it. "The women's movement is very strong in Jamaica," he says. "They have been able to start a debate about domestic violence. From a pastoral perspective, it is very important that we work both with women who have been victims and abusive men on the one hand, and with men and women in general on the other. Many men feel that they are not valued and feel completely defeated by the enormous social changes, caused particularly by unemployment. Frustrated by being unable to fulfill the mandate of providing for his family and feeling marginalized in his own home, a man may express this by beating his spouse, who in many cases is the one who is supporting the family. We also find that young men frequently beat their girlfriends. This is because they feel unable to cope with the demands placed on them by women to be financially successful. Many young men, on reaching adolescence, no longer have a place in their home, since they are pushed out if they cannot find work to help support the family. This creates anguish and aggressiveness."

The seminary curriculum now includes training on domestic violence for pastors and lay people. Hilary Nicholson of Women's Media Watch has organized workshops both at the seminary and with people from the grassroots in the inner cities. Women's Media Watch also organizes discussion and training sessions to make people aware of the issue of violence in the media and to help them critically to analyze the messages emitted by the media.

Many pastors are also receiving training in mediation and conflict resolution. Donna Parchment, an attorney who works for Dispute Resolution, says that mediators and counsellors trained by her organization are already working in nine of the fourteen parishes into which Jamaica is divided administratively. "It is important to show that there are other ways of responding to conflict," says Donna Parchment. "People should be aware that they can achieve important changes in conflict situations by using mediation techniques that help to overcome the barriers caused by division and confrontation." Dispute Resolution also conducts training programmes for police officers and for high school and university teachers and students. A special concern of the organization is the situation in Jamaican prisons, particularly the high-security institutions. To respond to the many violent situations Dispute Resolution has conducted three workshops to teach prison guards about the peaceful resolution of disputes.

The Jamaica Council of Churches (JCC), which has 11 member churches, has been working with the Ministry of Health to create shelters for women and children victims of violence. It has also developed special programmes for low-income children. Rev. Norman Mills, general secretary of the JCC, believes that the increasing number of children at risk and the growth in cases of domestic violence in recent years makes it imperative for the churches to work together in this area. In several Jamaican cities ministers from various churches have begun to work together on social issues under the umbrella of an organization known as the Ministers' Fraternal. More than once, the ministers have gone together to a neighbourhood in conflict to speak publicly with the residents about their problems and to talk with the gang leaders. The latter do not always listen to them, particularly if they are involved in the drug trade and have thus achieved a level of economic power. Nevertheless, the ministers are willing to launch campaigns in their churches and neighbourhoods against the use of drugs, encouraging young people to lead lives free of addiction.

The churches have also inaugurated an annual Day of Prayer for Peace on the second Sunday of December, which brings together thousands of people in a prayer vigil to support all efforts aimed at the peaceful resolution of conflict in Jamaican neighbourhoods.

Garrett Roper, a layman from the First Missionary Church and an advisor to the government on development and youth, is convinced that the churches must continue to uncover and denounce the deep economic roots that provoke violence. "Violence in the inner cities is nourished mainly by political manipulation, negligence on the part of the authorities and a lack of economic opportunities," he says. "There is a 'revolver culture' among us, which is reinforced by the messages from the media. It is essential that the churches and society work for a change of mentality in favour of peace and not violence, raising awareness about it and facing the cultural roots of violence." The divisions between the different Christian denominations and confessions do not help the work for peace, Garrett Roper says. "We need to be self-critical. We churches should have a joint witness in the face of violence. If we can do that, I think we will be able to build a history of peace and justice for Jamaica."

9. Towards a Culture of Peace

How is peace in a city visible? Is it only in the absence of confrontation and death in the streets? Or is there a special climate of peace that one can detect, mirrored in the lives and faces of the people?

The stories shared through the Peace to the City campaign of the World Council of Churches provide some important clues. People have come together – as individuals and in groups including churches and other religious bodies – to respond to situations of extreme violence with nonviolent efforts to find solutions. Dialogue, advocacy for civil rights, community development, analysis, action, reconciliation – these and other elements help to build a culture of peace by bringing about a cessation of immediate violence and by addressing the causes of violence in order to prevent further tragedy and build communities of peace with justice.

In the Rio das Pedras area of Rio de Janeiro, people were able to overcome division, prejudice and fear by working together in building new houses. Groups of neighbours chose names for these houses which expressed their hope in the new possibilities opened up to them in the neighbourhood they were building. In Majesty Garden in Kingston, the new houses built by the residents through a self-help system stood out because of their completely different appearance. Not only were they not separated by any type of fence, but they were painted, clean and well-kept, with curtains in the windows and hand-made runners on the tables. Recovering their right to adequate housing, and in the process their dignity, had changed the climate in which the population lived. Peaceful coexistence, tested by sharing equally the tasks involved in building houses, was shown to be possible. A similar phenomenon can be seen in Bambhayi, in Durban. The residents are proud of having worked together to build the bridge at the entrance to the settlement. This project also tested their capacity to accept each other regardless of differing political affiliations and convictions so that they could accomplish their task in peace. In so doing, they regained respect for themselves and also for others.

How can one put a stop to escalating violence? The situations portrayed in the preceding seven chapters can involve so much tension and can be so threatening that no one has the time or capacity to theorize about peace. What is important, as the achievements in these seven cities show, is to carry out actions to build peace. These actions involve the intervention of mediators, of facilitators, of people who encourage dialogue between the different parties, as well as of individuals who can console, sustain and accompany the victims of conflict and those who must make decisions related to it. People need to be trained at different levels of responsibility in this work for peace.

Often this training is provided in places far away from the conflict. People from violent contexts in Belfast, Durban and Kingston have been invited to participate in meetings outside the community in which daily confrontation takes place, so that they can analyze their situation in an environment that allows them to be more objective and to reflect independently. Corrymeela in Northern Ireland, the Valley of the Thousand Hills in Kwazulu Natal, Jamaica's Blue Mountains – all offer the distance from harsh reality which gives people space to begin to think about changes in behaviour, about coming closer together, about negotiating peace. Children, young people and adults can take part in experiments that help them to analyze their own behaviour and envisage the kind of changes in themselves and their communities that will be needed to improve the situation.

Equality, civil rights and regaining dignity as individuals must be tangible, as the experience in several cities has shown. In the Rights Counters that operate in several *favelas* in Rio de Janeiro, people sense that they are being helped not out of charity for them as victims but out of respect for their rights as citizens. When community representatives met at the Codman Square centre in Boston to discuss the conflicts and low academic level at the Dorchester high school, they were sure of their role as parents and students. They were demanding safety in the schools and better education not as a favour but as their right. When villagers in Batticaloa, Sri Lanka, insisted that they be allowed to go about their daily lives without being threatened by opposing forces, they did so not as victims, but as citizens whose rights have to be respected even by the armed forces. In Suva, a similar level of citizen awareness was evident in the efforts of the Citizens' Constitutional Forum to articulate people's demands for a constitutionally strong, multi-ethnic and multi-cultural society.

The experience of work for peace in these seven cities also shows that people also need symbolic acts through which to express peace. In Rio de Janeiro, the two minutes of silence by a population dressed in white on a Friday in December dynamized a great movement for inclusiveness and social peace. In Colombo, the 10,000 participants in a peace vigil, representing all of Sri Lanka's religious groups and dozens of organizations working for the common good, encouraged each other's commitment to negotiations for peace between the parties in conflict. In Suva, the work of People's Intercultural Awareness in combining the welcoming ceremonies of the Indo-Fijian and indigenous Fijian cultures sends a clear message that coexistence and respect for each other's values are possible. In Belfast, the fact that Catholics and Protestants could end a day spent together at Dromontine with a meditation on the Bible, songs and prayers is a signal of respect and recognition of the freedom of others to express their identity and religious faith.

"Problems are resolved as the community begins to work together," says one of the leaders working for peace in Boston's inner city. The experience common to all these seven cities is that wherever and whenever people from different backgrounds and from different decision levels are willing to work together, they can find solutions to growing violence. To do so requires a sense of vocation and considerable courage, but also an open mind, adequate training and the conviction that working for peace cannot be separated from working for justice and equal opportunities. When a community adopts these values and puts them into practice, it is possible to build the foundations for a culture of peace.